Green Card Marriage

Martyna Dearing

To request permissions, contact the publisher at drewsbookstoreva@gmail.com
Paperback: 979-8-9889899-0-5
Ebook: 979-8-9889899-1-2

First paperback edition published in March 2020.

Edited by Georgina Tsang
Cover art by Jane Farrell
Cover photograph by Evan Lane
Illustration by Courtney Paige Boyd
Interior layout by Martyna Dearing

Printed by IngramSpark

Published by
Drew's Bookstore
70 Main St, suite 22
Warrenton, VA 20186

drewsbookstoreva@gmail.com
drewsbookstore.com

Green Card Marriage

Martyna Dearing

To Drew,
for driving 2 hours in the middle of the night
all the way to DC... just to meet that cute Tinder girl.

To Georgina (Gina),
the best underpaid editor in the history of self-publishing.

To Nerea (Lola),
my toughest critic and my favorite backup soulmate.

To Andy,
the only person who showed up at my very first book signing.
you are the reason I still believe.

MARTYNA & ANDREW's

LOVE STORY

Contents

Author's Note

Here I am, pulling a Taylor Swift. I published this book about 3 years ago and honestly…? It's been bothering me a lot. Let's start with the fact that yes, English is not my first language. Still, the number of spelling and grammar mistakes was insane. How did anyone let me publish such a raw edit? I knew it wasn't perfect, but it wasn't until I reread it and then opened it in Grammarly that I realized it was way worse than I ever imagined.

Another thing is the way it was published. I was a young, inexperienced author and had ZERO ideas about writing or publishing a book. While I'm incredibly proud of becoming a published author, that joy was kind of taken away from me by a company named Writers Republic. They took my money, wanted to take even more, and never came through with any promises they made. As far as I know, there was no real marketing plan in place. And have I mentioned how they let me publish it? With numerous spelling and grammar mistakes. They did something I could've done all on my own but charged me over $1,000 for it. Technically, it wasn't a scam, my book got published. But at the same time, it kind of was. Since, after the first check (a very small, tiny check), I never saw my royalties again.

For the past three years, I haven't gotten over the fact that they were in charge of publishing and distributing my book. "Green

Card Marriage" is my firstborn baby and that will never change, so I'm doing it. I'm pulling a Taylor Swift and taking ownership of my work. I refuse to give another penny to those sharks, who are using poor inexperienced authors to make money off them. It's disgusting.

Lastly, my name. I remember going back and forth about whether I should publish under my maiden or married name. I went with my maiden name and I remember Andrew being kind of upset about it. I told him it was the last thing I could ever do under my maiden name and that's how I wanted it to be published. Three years later, I'm glad I did it. Not because of some weird nostalgia for my Polish name. It's mostly because I get to fix all of my mistakes and come back stronger and wiser as Martyna Dearing.

Don't get me wrong, Martyna Nowacka was awesome, but she was young, naive, and definitely inexperienced. She didn't know much about love and definitely couldn't pick her battles. She thought she had something to prove to the world, even to her husband.

Am I now talking in the third person? Oh boy… Let's fix that. The first year of our marriage was difficult and painful. It wasn't Andrew's or my fault, it just seemed like everything was against us. We came out so good, though. We finally reached the point when we learned how to communicate and appreciate each other… then life struck again. But that's another story.

I re-read those pages today and I see the chapter titled "How to Get Used To Being No One?" and my heart aches. Writing this book helped me find my voice again. It was actually my first attempt to write anything in a very long time and ever since, I've never stopped writing. It took me even longer to realize I didn't need to be all "Miss Independent" in my relationship with Andrew to be a strong independent woman at the same time.

I don't think I actually got it fully right until it was too late.

That's why this version has a couple of major updates. One, not only is the author Martyna Dearing but also, my name in the book is no longer spelled Martina. I'm over the phase of misspelling my name. Probably should've thought about that before I got the "MartinaTravels" tattoo…

Two! Aaron Douglas is Andrew Dearing, and Andrew Dearing is Aaron Douglas. I guess I wanted to be cool and avoid his name being out in the open just in case I got famous, but that clearly didn't happen. At this point in my life, I want everyone to know his name. Andrew Dearing, the love of my life. There's no reason for changing his name to anything else because I need people to know our story. I want everyone to know Andrew. He deserves to be known.

So today, it is my pleasure to share this updated version of Green Card Marriage with you. I fixed everything that I felt needed to be fixed and possibly added a few paragraphs here and there since I'm much smarter and way funnier these days. I didn't rewrite the story, though. It sounds much better now and it might be slightly spicier than it was before but at the end of the day, it's the same book.

While I don't feel the same way about many things I put on paper over 3 years ago - who am I to tell that version of me that her words weren't right or that her feelings were not valid?

I was hurt, and angry. I was frustrated, and extremely homesick for London. At the same time, I was madly in love, which I had never envisioned myself being. I was only 23… Every word in this book came from my heart. I poured my 23-year-old soul onto the paper and I don't regret it even for a minute. I see this story a bit differently now but I'd never dare to tell younger Martyna that she wasn't right to feel and write everything the way she did. I wish I could tell her it's all going to be okay, but I'd be lying.

Instead, if I got a chance to talk to my younger self I'd say:

"Stop being stupid and appreciate him. You don't know how much time together you have left."

To anyone who has purchased the Martyna Dearing version (winky face, if you know, you know)... thank you so much! It means the world to me, you don't even know. Still, I'm not republishing my work because I'm expecting any kind of profit from it. I'm republishing it because it feels right.

Part of me doesn't want to republish this book. The last thing I want to do is to burn the bridges I've worked so hard to rebuild over the past 3 years. I'm risking a lot by telling my truth, again. However, every time I reconsider this decision, the writer in me fights back.

"This is your story. Why the hell are you so afraid to share it?"

Love,

Martyna Dearing

Introduction

My story is very simple. At least it would be in an ideal world. There was a girl, she met a boy, they fell in love and now they're getting married. So nice, right?! Well, there's only one little catch.

I am an immigrant.

There, I said it. I hate this word because right away it feels wrong. Like I am someone worse than my American fiancé. Like I'm less of a human just because I wasn't born in this country and now I want to stay here.

Believe me when I say that the United States of America is definitely not my favorite country in the world. It's probably in the top 10, but still, I would never bother that much just to be able to live here. At least that's what I thought until I met him. Andrew freaking Dearing turned my life upside down and sometimes I really hate him for that. But most of the time, I'm just madly in love with him, and that makes me freak out even more.

If you reach for this book, be prepared to get a bit of a love story. Also, be prepared for me to complain a lot about the American system or just the whole country. You might even get some heartbreaks going on. Perhaps drama…

What you're definitely not getting is a perfectly written book. I'm not gonna hide it, English is not my first language and it'll never be. The whole purpose of me sharing this story with you is to show you my struggles with living in a foreign country. So yes, my grammar is not perfect. My wording might be off sometimes. Maybe some sentences will sound a bit funny. You might have to read some things twice to actually get it. But after all, does it really matter? If it does, maybe my story is not for you after all. According to the love of my life, my improper English is cute.

No Boys Allowed

If you'd asked me about marriage and all that stuff when I was 10, I'd tell you I never wanted to get married. Damn, if you asked me two years ago my answer would still have been exactly the same.

My whole life I knew I was meant for something great and I was not afraid to share that thought. Being raised in a small town in Poland didn't stop me from dreaming big. It did cause me many years of bullying and people laughing at my ideas. But I didn't care… Well, actually I was crying my eyes out for most of my teenage years but that's not the point. The point is, I never gave up.

I was born a redhead, even though my whole family had dark blonde hair. Believe it or not, but that already gave me a terrible head start. It's ridiculous to think that in a world where people are fighting racism and hate crimes, someone could be discriminated against for being ginger. Well, is it though? Welcome to Poland, where being a redhead is the worst social crime to be committed.

Kids would laugh at me, teachers would make mean jokes, and even my friends were cruel sometimes. I wouldn't be able to even count how many times I heard things like:

“You’ve got no soul, you’re a redhead!”

“If we were in the Middle Ages you’d be burnt on a pyre.”

“If you weren’t ginger you could’ve been pretty.”

“Redheads are not allowed to have an opinion.”

“The worst thing that could ever happen to me would be having a ginger kid.”

Imagine your whole life being bullied by everyone. Sometimes even your closest friends or family. I grew into hating Poland and Polish people just because of the way they treated me. Being an adult now I see how stupid it was and I can appreciate my country after all. But I know one thing for sure… I’ll never go back.

After leaving high school, I lived my life free from all the discrimination I’d seen and experienced, and I was very happy to leave Poland behind. I traveled a lot. First, I moved to the USA and became an au pair. Then I came back to Europe, got a summer job in Greece, and moved back to Poland just to realize it was a huge mistake. So I headed to London where I lived and worked for over a year. Then flew back to the States.

In between all of this, there was no room for boys. I never had a real boyfriend, unless you count those from elementary school. I never told anyone I loved them. I lost my virginity with a friend I didn’t even like that much, just so I wouldn’t have to worry about it later. At the same time, high school boys treated me like the plague because.. well, because I was a redhead and apparently that made me extremely ugly and undesirable.

I never expected falling in love so hard. I’ve always been a huge romantic, but I also knew that the movie kind of love didn’t happen a lot. I accepted that it would never happen to me and I was completely okay with it. I was so happy to travel and explore the world. I had a plan and there was no room for boys in it. No time for love. No willingness to settle down.

And that’s probably why meeting Andrew hit me so hard. He appeared in my life out of nowhere. Of course, he had perfect timing. Just when I was ready for something more than an occasional hook-up, but before any other guy could use that opportunity.

I fell in love quickly and deeply and somehow he decided to stick around and make me do the same. Before I knew it, my life turned into a romantic comedy, and every time I watched people falling in love on the screen I'd think:

"I have that kind of love. I'm just as lucky."

I always knew I was meant for great things but I never thought I was meant for great love. Out of all the things I imagined for myself as a kid or teenager, being a wife was definitely not one of them.

However, I found a person who is completely and absolutely in love with me. I moved to a country that accepted me, and I found friends who taught me how to love myself. Almost every single day I'm asked where my accent is from. When I reply, people only smile and say they love it.

That bullied kid I used to be would be so damn impressed with what we've achieved so far. I can imagine her excitement when she'd hear about us living in the US and marrying a super hot light-skinned guy. And to all the boys who thought I wasn't good enough for them… I proudly get hotter every year just for you (only half joking).

The Basics of Being an Au Pair

What is Au Pair in America?

The program is quite old. It was founded in the 20th century. The basic idea of the program is to send young international girls, between the ages of 18-26, to the United States as childcare providers. It's a live-in situation where host families decide to give the girls accommodation, food, and other things for a year in return for their work.

Besides all the live-in perks, all the girls get "pocket money". The amount is dependent on which type of program you participate in, but it's usually $200 a week. Rarely, it might be $250 - but $200 is the most typical salary for an au pair. Although, we are not allowed to call it a salary because we are not allowed to work.

Sounds a bit weird? Well, yes… The government is not okay with claiming au pairs as legal workers in the USA. That way, we are never allowed to have any other "job" than being "nannies" for our host families. We can only be au pairs.

So the government doesn't agree to call au pairs workers. They don't give us work permits. In their eyes, we are only "exchange visitors" and get "pocket money", so we have no rights as employees. Because again, technically we're not employed. See where I'm going with this? However, they have absolutely no issue with taxing our "pocket money" just like they tax all legally employed Americans.

What do au pairs do? We live with a host family, we take care of their kids, and we travel in between. We get two weeks of paid time off per year and then we can travel for a month after the program.

A lot of au pairs work with babies. Some of us would work with older kids. Depending on the age of the children, the responsibilities vary. Every au pair experience is different, every schedule is different. Every host family and every au pair are different as well.

Some host families are amazing. Some au pairs are horrible. Some schedules are tough and some are very easy.

You can't go to a completely different country and assume that everything will be okay. There will be a lot of ups and downs. With this program though, I'd say that 90% of our experience depends on the host family we choose to live with.

I've heard so many stories about both - crazy au pairs and crazy host families. As you might expect, the au pair program gets all of the nationalities, all of the cultures, and all of the crazy people. It gets amazing people as well. It's just a mix of everyone and everything. Sometimes it's an amazing mix and sometimes it's not.

There's no perfect au pair experience but there are a lot of good ones. My first year as an au pair was really great. My host family loved me, and they helped me a lot. Sometimes they abused my kindness and willingness to help. But honestly, I didn't mind because they were kind and helpful to me as well.

You see, a huge part of an au pair experience is based on the host family. If you feel unwelcome in the house you live in, it's gonna be a tough year. You can say I experienced both sides of this program. The amazing one is when you love everyone and keep in touch for years afterward and the sad one is when you don't want to see them ever again.

Manchester

Three years ago, when I wrote this book, I was kind of too afraid of what people would say and too inexperienced to do this story justice. That's why I've decided this is the one chapter that needs to be re-written. The truth is that Manchester was the poster child for a Fuckboy. Well, poster man. Poster... boy? You know what I mean. It took me a few years, loads of relationship podcasts, and countless stories from other girls to understand that. But today, it's loud and clear.

He was 29, I think, and I was 20. It's quite funny how back then he seemed so grown up and mature. Yet, here I am, about to turn 27, and not even close to being either of those things. He was incredibly handsome and had a deep sexy voice and a British accent. I mean, how can you expect a 20-year-old not to fall for that? The first time we saw each other outside of work was at the office party, and we just argued about everything. He was rude and arrogant. And that was hot. He contradicted everything I said, but not in a jerk way, in an "I'm smarter than you way". Which I guess is also being a jerk. But he was older and was willing to talk to me about philosophy and stuff… let's just say I was so intellectually stimulated that I ended up waking up in his bed two weeks later.

I remember the first time he touched me at that office party. He gently put his hand on my knee. That's when I realized that this much older guy was interested in me. I pretended not to notice. I thought I had the power. I looked very proper and business-like. I knew if he saw me in my regular clothes, he'd be way more into me. I was drunk on the attention I was getting from this guy who was clearly way out of my league. Well, the truth is I was also just very drunk.

The next day I got my first email from him at work. My heart skipped a beat. Little did I know it would be doing that for another year, every time I saw his name popping up on my screen. For different reasons. Or maybe the same reason… I was just too scared to admit it.

One time he went on a work trip to Poland and promised to bring back my favorite snacks. When he got back, I emailed him something like:

"Thank you so much. I own you!"

Yes, I own you. Not owe, own. It wasn't even a spelling mistake, I just didn't know the difference, since at that time I was still learning English.

He proceeded to send me a screenshot of the definition of owning someone. Sexually. And at that moment, 20-year-old me could not have been more embarrassed. But at the same time, I was sure that this man wanted to sleep with me.

It was so hot. At least I thought it was. He would email me at work on a daily basis. I knew that if anyone found out we would probably get fired but that's what was so thrilling about it.

If you asked me now, that's when I lost my power. Or maybe I never even had it. I felt so embarrassed and uncertain about my language skills and life experience. Now I know that these things made it easier to trick me into thinking there was something between us, when there was nothing more than sexual tension.

One thing led to another, and he invited me for a date.

Surprise, surprise, it was incredibly far from my place, yet incredibly close to his. There's no way an older version of me would go for that but somehow 20-year-old Martyna was too excited about being asked on a date to see it as a red flag. Before I knew it, the tube was shut down and I was on the other side of London from my flat. Although, I'm actually not sure if it was closed - he definitely told me it was.

He obviously suggested staying at his place until the tube opened up. [Un]surprisingly, he was not okay with me leaving in the morning after we had sex (at that time, the best sex of my life). Everything he did made me feel like this was more than a one night stand. He begged me to stay. We spent half a day tangled in his sheets. He walked me to the tube after 1 PM and then he kissed me and said:

"See you at work."

And that was it.

Somehow, he managed to ghost me despite us working in the same building. For months, he acted like nothing ever happened. I was mad and frustrated but at the same time still very much into him. I didn't know any better. If I did, I wouldn't have let him pull the same shit again...

He invited me out again, a whole year later. I agreed, just to prove a point. I had a plan. I chose the sexiest dress I had in the closet. A red spaghetti strap mini dress. I wore black high-heeled booties with a leather jacket on top. I looked amazing and I knew it. The plan was to make him realize what he lost, and then leave.

But how do you leave a guy who's driving you crazy? And when all you want him to do is to just shut up and put you against the wall? I didn't leave. I stayed.

I was sitting on his balcony, drinking whiskey and admiring a view of East London. At some point, he laughed:

"C'mon! You must realize you're not the prettiest girl I've ever dated! I've been with many girls way hotter than you. You're still awesome, though."

I was sure he wasn't lying, but to hear something like that from a guy I was really into… well, it hurt like hell. However, I wanted to be that cool girl who didn't care. So I smiled and pretended like he had every right to point that out.

A few hours later, I realized that when I had changed into my way-too-short mini dress in the office bathroom, I left my house keys there. I wouldn't be able to get them back till Monday.

I called all of my flatmates but it was the middle of the night and no one picked up. So I stayed because I had a flight to Norway in about four hours. We had sex, we smoked weed, we drank more whiskey and then he ordered me an Uber to the airport.

See, I had decided to prove my theory. All you need to travel is your wallet and a phone. As long as you have your ID and money, you can go anywhere (at least in Europe).

That's how I ended up doing a walk of shame in an insanely short red mini dress and high heels, smelling like whiskey, through airport security. Then I proceeded to get a toothbrush, clean underwear, and a new dress. Plus a very cute backpack and a carry-on suitcase from the Cath Kidston store at Heathrow. That suitcase is still my favorite piece of luggage that holds more memories than my brain ever could.

I met my cousin in Norway, and we spent 24 hours together before I flew back to London. As soon as I landed, I texted Manchester. We had two weeks until I was leaving London and I was going to use that time well.

We kept sleeping with each other until my last day at the office. The sex was amazing. The feeling that he was into me was probably even better. As I walked to the office that last day, half an hour late… I still believed there was something more to it. Technically I knew the only reason why we were doing it was because I was leaving and he knew he would never have to see me again. But part of me still hoped this wasn't the end.

He was the only guy who came to my goodbye party which made everything that much more awkward. And again, made me feel… special, I guess? I mean he knew what he was doing.

He knew everyone would know why he was there and he still showed up. That had to mean something, right? But now, I don't think it did.

He walked me to the tube and that was the last time I saw him. I expected a grand goodbye, any kind of emotion showing me it wasn't all in my head. Instead, I got:

"Hope you find an American guy and get married!"- I'm not lying, he really said that.

And guess what? That's exactly what I did. I found someone who never, not even once, made me doubt I was the most beautiful girl in the room.

After saying goodbye to him on Friday night and crying my eyes out for about three hours, I got off my bed, took a deep breath, and started packing. I had the best last weekend in London running one last race, meeting up with some friends, and sending more and more packages as I realized I couldn't fit a whole room into a suitcase.

I got into an airplane on Monday morning and smiled when we took off.

So thank you, Manchester. You gave me a very valuable lesson. You showed me what real love could never be.

Welcome to America, Baby!

When my host family asked me to come back for another year, I didn't hesitate even for a moment. I knew that another Great American Adventure was exactly what I needed.

Don't get me wrong, I loved living in London but at the same time I was kind of lonely. I didn't have real friends to hang out with, and all my colleagues from work had their partners or friend groups already. I was dating... a lot. But to be fair, I wasn't interested in any kind of relationship because I knew I wanted to travel the world. I didn't need anyone to hold me back in any way.

So after the whole Manchester drama, I got on a plane and moved back to the US.

Every au pair spends her first days at the orientation in the New York area. It kind of gives you time to settle in and realize it's really happening. That you're going to spend your next year in the States, make your American Dream come true, blah, blah, blah...

For me, it was my second time as an au pair and with the same host family so I felt pretty confident and treated the whole thing as a great opportunity to make some new friends. I had so much fun and expected just the whole year to go nicely and smoothly. I had a plan for everything and wasn't expecting any surprises. I was going to travel a lot, save some money and, after the program, leave for Asia for a year to volunteer as an English teacher or something like that. What could go wrong?

On the train from the Orientation to DC, I was ecstatic. All the girls seemed great, we already exchanged numbers and were planning on spending the 4th of July together. I remember thinking:

"This is gonna be the most amazing year of my life."

And oh, boy… it was. But for completely different reasons than I thought it would be. It would also be the most exhausting and nerve-wracking year for me. That was completely unexpected. I remember sitting on that train in a pink dress which was as old as the kids I was about to take care of. It seems amazing how much has changed in just a bit over a year since then. I'll always appreciate every experience no matter how bad it was. I'm proud of the person I am right now. But part of me will always miss that girl in the pink dress from the train. Because once she got off, nothing was ever the same.

Kirsten

Kirsten played a huge part in my life, especially within the last couple of years. A lot of people might see Kirsten as a villain, and sometimes I would even agree with you, but it would be very unfair from my side to include only the bad parts about her. That's what this description is for. Most of my stories will be telling you that she was an alcoholic, she hated the fact I had a boyfriend or a fiancé, and she made me feel unwelcome in the house I used to call home. However, it's only one side of Kirsten that I knew.

Kirsten was very small but feisty. She was in her 50s and you could see that people respected her. She used to work on Wall Street and now she was crushing her job in DC. She was definitely smart and very pretty. I think that a lot of men in her business would have underestimated her because of her looks, but then she always made sure to prove them wrong. I was always admiring her for being so successful.

I also admired her for taking care of the whole family when her husband was never there. She paid the bills, and supervised me and the kids to make sure they were always ready for school. She would manage their playdates and school activities. Most importantly she sacrificed all of her free time to make her daughter happy. She would get up at 4 AM every weekend and drive Mary, my host sister, to the court for tennis lessons or tournaments. Mary was an amazing kid, very active and talented but also very spoiled and difficult. The fact that Kirsten would do all of that for her without getting back any kind of gratitude was sad but even more admirable.

For a very long time, I considered her as a second mother. She was someone I could rely on and who'd help me any time I needed it. I still can't believe how it all went down...

Lola

Lola is very different from all the girls I usually hang out with. She hates shopping, and she always wears very basic clothes that don't reflect her personality at all. And believe me when I say... It's intense! Somehow she manages to pull off an outfit made up of pants that look like they are taken straight out of the boys' clothing section, and a Victoria's Secret bodysuit underneath. One time she made a porn video (her dancing on the bed and doing different sexy poses in another VS bodysuit) and sent it to me. Just in the middle of the week. During work hours. For no reason.

She's quite vulgar and because of her, the quality of my vocabulary dropped a few levels down for sure. She says things that would never come out of my mouth and she's the most confident person I've ever met. She's also the person who taught me that it's okay to say,

"I don't care what you think, I'm amazing."

Plus she added "dick" to my vocabulary.

I'll always admire her for her amazing Tinder profile. It's a perfect mix of self-confidence with a cockiness that, unfortunately, is mostly reserved for guys. She basically says:

"You can't handle me but I dare you to try."

Also, she's the one who made me skinny dip in the Atlantic Ocean in the middle of January at 35 degrees. She's the one who made me skinny dip again, this time in the Potomac River in April. And she's the one who jumped all alone into the National Mall basin, made us take amazing sunrise photos of her, and posted them as her Tinder profile pictures - all without getting any STDs or weird rashes from that disgusting water. I'd say it's pretty impressive.

Lola definitely became my best friend for life very quickly. We met on a train from the Orientation and have been stuck with each other ever since. About ten minutes after meeting me and the other au pairs, she was ready to share with us all the details of her sex and love life, so how could we not hit it off?

She stole my heart with her craziness and made me the person I am right now. When I came back to the US I felt a bit lonely, a bit confused, and definitely very far away from being confident in my life choices. She inspired me to believe in myself and take charge of my self-doubting mind once and for all. She made me proud of myself. And for that, I will always be thankful.

Also, her boobs are absolutely amazing and I have no idea how keeping them under all of those hoodies is legal. One day she'll burn in hell for hiding them like that. And I'll burn with her for all the inappropriate things we've done together.

This Is Why We Can't Have Nice Things

The 4th of July was great! I spent most of the day with Lola, my new Spanish friend, and we had so much fun together. We had brunch, went to the White House, and saw the parade. At that time we had already noticed we were getting along with each other pretty well. But Lola was underage so she went home afterward and I met up with another friend, Patricia, in order to search for parties.

Honestly, it was a disaster. While Lola and I were similar in so many ways, Patricia couldn't get me less. She was Brazilian and her style of partying was basically making guys buy us drinks.

All while being lesbian and constantly talking about how deeply she hated men. I'm sorry but I'd rather pay for my own alcohol than make any guy feel like I owe them something because they spent $10 on me.

While Patricia was on a mission to financially abuse all men in the bar, I was in my post-Manchester rebound phase.

The first part of the night I obviously had to spend wallowing about how no one was interested in me. Then, when we finally sat down to watch the fireworks on some random lawn somewhere in DC, I started chatting to some random guy. He was hot and could hold a conversation, so he basically checked all the boxes I had at that time. After the fireworks we proceeded to a bar where we found ourselves in a very heated conversation about... World War II? My point was: stupid men with their stupid guns. I went on and on about how no one should ever have access to guns, and how anyone even slightly engaging in wars was encouraging them. He argued with me, and I found that really hot and intellectually stimulating. But he conveniently forgot to mention he was a military guy.

He was ordering an Uber for Patricia, and I insisted he shouldn't be paying for it but then he said:

"No worries, I get a big discount."

"You get an Uber discount? How?" - I asked, completely clueless.

"Military." - he replied.

And suddenly it all became clear. I had spent over an hour telling a military guy how pointless and wrong his job was. Lesson learned. Know your audience before you decide to passionately share your views.

That didn't stop him from sleeping with me, though. I mean, I shit-talked all of his beliefs and values, but at least I'm pretty, right?

I got back home in the middle of the night and the house alarm went off. I drunkenly tried to turn it off, but it still woke my host mom up.

"Sorry," I whispered apologetically. "I was watching a movie at my friend's."

She didn't believe me, I knew it. But she didn't say anything and went back to sleep.

*****

What happened the next day was unexpected. It was my host brother's birthday. I spent all day with my host family, trying to prove I'm not that crazy au pair who came back home at 3 AM from a one-night stand. Josh and his dad went for a boat trip with their friends and I stayed with Mary and her mom to help out with a playdate.

Everything was okay until we came back home after dinner, when the girls went upstairs to play and I stayed in the living room with my host mom to chat. She was already a couple of glasses of wine in, which was a bit weird since I'd never noticed her drinking before. You could say she was a bit tipsy, at least I felt that way. Nothing to be concerned about… until she started crying and telling me how my host dad used to cheat on her.

It was my first week of being back as an au pair and the first thing my host mom told me when we were alone was their family drama. She started complaining she didn't love him anymore, she wasn't happy, and she wanted to leave him but she couldn't because of the kids. She was asking if I'd be there for her if she left him and I just didn't know what to say. She kept on crying and telling me all the details about my host dad's affair. I was so incredibly uncomfortable in that moment. I was very concerned about her too.

The summer went on and everything seemed to be quite okay, but I still couldn't forget about what my host mom told me that day. However, I really liked my host dad, so I decided to ignore the whole conversation.

One day he came up to me and asked me if his wife had been drinking. I said that she had a couple of glasses of wine and I asked why he needed to know that.

"See, Kirsten has some alcohol issues. She doesn't know when to stop. She shouldn't be drinking at all. Next time you see her drinking, could you stop her or at least let me know?"

That was crazy!

First of all, he expected me to stop a woman who was 30 years older than me from drinking. She was my employer too! What did he expect me to say to her? Plus, I really didn't see the issue. She had a few glasses of wine from time to time… so what?

Everyone does that. I just assumed it was a typical man telling a woman what she could and what she couldn't do.

I very quickly realized that I was the one who had it all wrong.

Back in London, I had sold my Taylor Swift concert tickets so I could afford my summer trips. So I was super excited to hear that Taylor Swift was coming to DC only a few weeks after my arrival! I was hoping that I might be able to convince my host mom to take me and Mary to the concert. Finally, on the day before the event, she got the tickets for all of us to go. I was beyond happy! I couldn't believe it was happening. We had great seats that were close to the stage and Kirsten paid for them. It couldn't get any better than that!

We ordered an Uber to the stadium since it was pretty far away. My host dad was standing on the porch all stressed out, looking like he was sending three daughters off to college. My host mom was acting a bit weird, though. She spent the whole ride trying to speak French to the driver (he mentioned his native language was French) and even I, without knowing the language that well, could hear that hers was terrible. I'm not gonna lie, I was embarrassed.

She was weirdly nice to him and there was just something very strange about her behavior, but I couldn't pinpoint what. We got out and headed straight to our seats. However, Kirsten needed to make a stop at the bar to get some wine. She got two cups, one for right away and the other one for later. The concert hadn't even started and she was already done with both. She also started dancing, and let's keep it real… embarrassed both me and her daughter in front of everyone. At that moment I knew that something was very wrong. She danced like she was high. I had known her for over three years and had never seen her dancing before. Ever.

She disappeared a few times saying she was going to the bathroom, but who knows where she was. The only thing I knew for sure was that I took Mary to get her a concert T-shirt, and when we came back, my host mom was gone. She kept calling me, screaming down the phone that she was waiting for us at our seats. She said we had left her and she was very angry with me.

The issue was that we were at our seats. And Kirsten was nowhere to be found.

It was a nightmare. It was so loud that she couldn't hear anything I was saying. Mary started freaking out. She was only 10 at the time and very scared for her mom. Her dad started calling us, asking what was happening. He asked with a very strict voice:

"Martyna, was Kirsten drinking?"

I almost cried when I confirmed that she was, in fact, drinking. I told him that I saw her drinking only two glasses of wine, but it seemed as though she was secretly getting drunk while "going to the bathroom".

I was terrified, and for some reason, I felt extremely guilty.

Kirsten continued calling me and her husband for a long time, screaming and being very angry with everyone. Finally, after about half an hour, she found us. Taylor had been on stage for only 20 minutes, but Mary said:

"I heard fireworks, I think they're done. Let's go home."

So, we headed home.

I didn't have any data on my phone so I couldn't order an Uber and Kirsten's phone wasn't working anymore. Also, she didn't have enough cash to get a cab. We ended up taking one home and then I had to pay the difference to be able to get out of the car. For the whole ride, she kept on saying it was the worst night of her life and it's all because we left her. I sat in silence and let her talk.

Then she passed out. My host dad had to carry her into the house. I told Mary her mom was just tired.

She never apologized. The next day everything went back to normal and she was just complaining she got lost at the concert and she'd never go to another one again.

Good Old Canada with an Aussie Twist

After all that host family drama I was ready to go off and enjoy some time on my own. The kids went to the camp for four weeks so I was very happy that everyone would get some time to rest. And full of hope that when I got back, everything would be back to how it used to be.

I flew to Vancouver and stayed there for a few days in a hostel. Amazing food, Irish bars, welcoming people, and stunning nature. Vancouver had it all.

It also had a bar crawl organized by my hostel. Very quickly I made some great friends and for the next two nights, we were partying our way through the city. It's truly amazing how at the age of 21 you can party all night and go hiking the next day.

Vancouver also had a cute Australian guy, Joel. He was the perfect rebound after Manchester. We went on a day tour together to see the Capilano Suspension Bridge which was fun. I wish I remembered all of our conversations but the truth is Joel wasn't that memorable besides the fact that we did it in a hostel bunk bed. That kind of adventure definitely got my mind off certain people.

After my "unforgettable" hostel stay, I joined a Trek America tour. Trek America was hands down my favorite tour company.

The tour leaders were always amazing, but this specific one exceeded all of my expectations. Will was different... He was this weird Australian guy (yes, clearly I went to Canada to have a thing for Aussie guys) with super long hair. He was completely not my type, but for some reason, he became my summer crush. Unlike Joel, I remember our conversations very well. And also unlike Joel, Will seemed to be immune to my charms. Instead, he won me over with his personality, lame jokes, and just being a friend when I needed it.

He was also an amazing tour leader. I'm not sure if I was clear enough about that in the survey the agency sent me after the tour. Based on what I wrote, they either thought he was the best tour leader in the world, or that we slept with each other. I probably went a bit too far in saying how amazing he was but to be fair, I did everything in my power to sleep with him and he kindly didn't take the hint. Even if in my modest opinion he was at least slightly interested in me. I mean, can you be more professional than that?

Will was the kind of guide who would walk us blindfolded to the viewpoint, just so we could experience seeing it without any spoilers. One time when I forgot my backpack at Tim Hortons, he drove me all the way back and we talked about traveling, not wanting to settle down, and all that stuff. I spent only a couple of weeks with him (and 10 other people), but some people leave a mark on us for life, even after such a short period of time. Every time I think of Will, I just remember the warm feeling of friendship. And the fact that he wouldn't sleep with me…

Most importantly, part of our group tour was Gina. Gina was the worst hiking buddy I've ever had, but also a great listener ready to hear all about my emotional disability. I told her everything about Manchester and my high school trauma. I definitely kept her posted about my feelings towards Will. Hiking with her would always take us double what it should, but I didn't mind. A great friendship was formed. Plus I got really cute pictures. Who would've known that our fake wedding planning and joking about some of the most ridiculous bridal ideas on one of our hikes would become so real just a year later…

Family Secrets

When I got back to DC, I was excited about the fresh start with my host family. I was sure that with no kids around my host mom finally had some time for herself, and we all could move past that weird phase.

Again, I couldn't be more wrong.

Once I got back home, Kirsten was drunk almost every single night. For me, the situation was even worse because I was having a friend over. We met at Orientation back in New York and she was visiting DC for a few days. I had invited her to stay with us before I knew what was happening with Kirsten.

Like the situation couldn't get any weirder, we had a dog called Clementine… she was the best part of living with my host family. I was totally in love with her. They got her during my first time as an au pair and I had taken care of her since she was a puppy. Once I came back, Clementine was obsessed with me. She never left my side, followed me everywhere, and stayed in the basement (where I lived) waiting for me in the dark for hours, just so she could see me when I got back. She was the most loyal dog I had ever had.

What was so weird about it? Well, Kirsten couldn't stand my bond with Clem.

Every time she got drunk, she would yell from her bedroom:

"Clementine, come!!! Clementine!!!" - I could hear her heavy drunken steps upstairs.

She would not let Clementine sleep with me. She forced her to come up the stairs and sleep in her bedroom. She'd close the doors to prevent Clem from running away.

Clementine was my dog. I raised her. I taught her not to pee in the house, and I was the only one taking her for walks. To this day, I get so frustrated with how Kirsten tried to separate us. She hated the fact that Clem didn't want to spend any time with her. She always 'joked' that I stole her dog.

Things took a bad turn when one night my friend was at our house. Kirsten started screaming and tried to take Clementine away from us.

My friend was very confused. She had no idea what was going on and kept asking why my host mom was freaking out so badly. I was so embarrassed and I didn't feel that telling her about Kirsten's drinking problem would help anyone. So I kept quiet and just explained that my host mom liked sleeping with the dog. But we both could feel the weirdness of the whole situation.

What was I supposed to say?

"Sorry, she's just a bit drunk..." ?!

I felt bad for Clementine and for my friend for putting her in that kind of situation. I felt very violated. I could handle drunk Kirsten in privacy but not in front of my friends. I always told everyone how amazing my host family was, and that night I felt like I was just lying to myself.

*****

Right before the kids came back from the camp, I tried to cook dinner for my host parents every night, so they could spend more time with each other... and possibly solve their issues. In all honesty, I was trying to fix something that I should have never been involved in in the first place. But they made it my problem.

One day, I was invited to eat with them.

Kirsten started with a glass of wine. My host dad was not very happy with it, but he said:

“Okay, just one glass.”

Halfway through dinner, she was completely drunk. She started crying that she didn’t know what to do, that she felt helpless, and that she hated everything. It was the most uncomfortable moment of my life. I wanted to feel bad for her, and I really did. But I also couldn’t take her seriously when I saw her messing with her food with a fork, dropping it from time to time, and behaving like a little kid.

She asked my host dad if she needed to eat everything, and for the first time, I saw how pathetic she was. I realized he was in charge of her. He had all the power. He was making all the decisions for her.

So the next time she asked for another glass of wine, he could easily have said “no” to her. He actually did, but then she just kept on begging, so after a few minutes he gave up and poured her one more. And then another one.

My mind was screaming. I couldn’t believe what was happening. It felt like I was in a movie because these people were not acting like the normal healthy family that I used to know. I felt so uncomfortable... I never wanted to see them again.

But, I also remembered the people I used to know. They helped me a lot. They were kind and were my home away from home. Every time I thought of leaving them, I instantly felt guilty and ashamed. What would people say? That I came to a perfect family, at least that’s what I was saying, and now I was leaving them for another one? That there was one little problem and I couldn’t handle it already. That would be selfish… and the kids needed me. I couldn’t leave the kids in that situation.

Everyone would hate me... so I stayed.

I told Lola though. I told her about everything. I think if it wasn't for her, I would've just left and come back to Europe. I feel thankful for her. She made me brave. She kept me going through hell, and she never told me what I wanted to hear.

One thing I know for sure, Lola has always been brutally honest with me. She never forced me to do anything, but she was never afraid of giving me her opinion either.

That's how she was with me every single time my host family made me upset. When I was coming to her crying that I couldn't take it anymore. She would also say all the things about Kirsten that I didn't want to say out loud. She'd call her the B word as many times as it took to make me feel better. She would complain to me, scream at me, and get offended on my behalf. She always had crazy ideas of what I should do to get my revenge when Kirsten started being really mean about my dating. Lola was the person who turned that terrible summer into one of the best ones (or craziest) of my life.

I will always love her for that.

Feeling 22

September was pretty uneventful. I went to Chicago to meet up with my Polish friend and discovered I hated her boyfriend - so while avoiding him, I slept with his brother. They also reassured me that I definitely never wanted to live in a Polish community again.

I lost my phone in an Uber and had to ask my host family to get me a new one which was very awkward, but fortunately, they did. It was also the time for me to take a break from partying since I was about to run a marathon in just a couple of months, so I focused mainly on that.

I realized Lola was definitely my best friend. We were getting super close and basically decided we were soulmates. Or a match made in hell... depending on who you asked.

Lola was very inappropriate and way too straight-forward for me. I found it amusing. She was still underage but that didn't stop us from drinking Jägermeister with ginger ale in my basement.

Everything started revolving around my birthday weekend in Nashville and that was the only thing I thought or talked about. We had been preparing for it since the very beginning of our au pair year, and finally, it was almost time to hit the road.

*****

I was always very big on my birthdays. I loved celebrating every holiday and my birthday was no exception. So it was no surprise that I forced all of my friends to go to Nashville with me to celebrate. I even invited someone I had known only for half an hour just because we needed one more person for the car. In the end, it turned out to be a great idea though. Aroa became a great friend very quickly. This trip started a long beautiful friendship.

We left on Thursday night and drove for 10 hours to get there on Friday morning. Lola couldn't come in the car because she had to stay at work, so she was supposed to fly over the next day. Also, she was super sick. I was kind of worried about whether she would be able to come at all.

Nashville was insanely fun. It's one of those places I could never live but have enjoyed every single time I visited. It's a place full of live music and of course, tourists. Everyone was here. Students, bachelorette parties, guys' weekends, 21st birthdays... anyone ready to party. It's kind of like Vegas but they decided to replace casinos with country bars. Plus, I'd kill to eat Honky Tonk's nachos any day.

My friend from Chicago came over as well. Unfortunately, she brought her boyfriend and his brother, and they stayed with us in the Airbnb.

Unsurprisingly, we got super drunk on the first night. In true Martyna style, I thought it was a great idea to get through the day with only a bit of nachos, go to sleep at 2 PM, then wake up at 7 AM, and proceed to eating a pack of butterscotch chocolate chips while emptying a bottle of wine.

Yeah… I woke up the next day throwing up my guts and wishing the weekend was already over. I picked up Lola from the airport. Apparently, she got some weed from her Uber driver in DC and by the time she got to Nashville she was completely high.

I, a person who had never purchased drugs before, had questions.

How did she even start a conversation leading up to getting weed from an Uber guy? No idea! The most important thing was that she didn't feel sick anymore. Apparently smoking marijuana cured her and the fever was gone.

Meanwhile, the little brother of the annoying boyfriend started getting very clingy and wanted to start something I wasn't feeling up for. Did we have a thing back in Chicago? Yes, barely. But I only slept with him because there was nothing better to do. We've all done this... right?

Very quickly, he became the most annoying person on that trip. He tried his best with every single girl and didn't succeed. He was two years younger than me and probably several years younger than the other girls. He had no chance. Mostly because he was acting like a kid and got way too drunk.

He and Lola were the only ones underage and since Lola and I were a package deal, I was with them by default. So we ended up stuck with him, putting his ass in an Uber and getting him back home safely. Meanwhile, everyone else was having the night of their lives...

I was tired, Lola was tired, and he was wasted. When we got back to the Airbnb, Lola and I decided to sleep on the couch so others could get the beds. And that's how we spent our only night together in Nashville. Believe it or not, we kind of had fun. After all, it was us. We always did.

On our last morning we went back to Honky Tonk, ordered the nachos for breakfast and requested "22" by Taylor Swift from the band. Lola and I danced our asses off in the middle of the bar at 11 AM, completely sober. And that was the best part of the whole weekend.

You Had Me at Wizards

After Nashville I was tired. I didn't enjoy partying as much as I wanted to and that kind of got to me. I had just turned 22 and for the first time I felt like I was tired of partying and meaningless hookups. I wanted something more.

That didn't necessarily mean a relationship but I wanted some kind of connection with another person. Friends with benefits at least...

Don't ask me why, but back in Nashville, I had downloaded Tinder again.

I hated Tinder. That's for sure. But also, as Lola would say, I was kind of emotionally disabled. I had no idea how to start a healthy relationship with a guy. I usually didn't have to worry about that because I was traveling too much to get settled down. But as I said, I was trying to change my habits a bit… so naturally I went on Tinder.

After a few days, I already hated it and stopped using it. But from time to time I'd start swiping again just to make sure I actually really hated it. Every time I came to the same conclusion - I did hate it.

Until, one day, I got matched with a super hot guy who was

definitely not my type and completely out of my league.

I usually liked blonde baby-faced guys, and he was anything but that.

Andrew was light-skinned (Afro American mixed with Caucasian) and very masculine. He looked tall in his pictures. I could see he exercised a lot. He had some hiking photos with no shirt on but nothing too in your face... and also a picture with a guitar. I was sold. That basically checked all of my boxes. He was sporty and played the guitar. What more could a girl want?

To be honest, I was totally surprised that he texted me first. I mean, really… he was waaaaay too hot for me. I read the message:

"You had me at Wizards"

It was a reply to my Tinder bio:

"Looking for a Wizards games buddy"

I smiled and replied, and the rest is history... Well, kind of.

I told him I loved ice cream for breakfast. He claimed that me loving basketball and desserts for the first meal of the day was too good to be true. He said I should just marry him right away. I joked I had a dress ready in my closet and we could do it the next day if he was up for it. We texted for hours before we finally gave in and went to sleep.

After that night we talked all the time for about a week and I was really into it. He was smart and funny. He definitely wasn't trying any weird moves that would have suggested there was a 40-year-old creep behind those cute photos.

He didn't really seem into the idea of meeting me, though. I tried a few times to get him out on a date but he lived super far away from me. I wasn't sure how we matched in the first place. My preferred distance on the app did not reach Virginia for sure. One time we had a date scheduled and he canceled on me at the last minute saying he had a headache. I was kind of discouraged but I liked talking to him too much to let him go just yet.

It was Halloween weekend, and I was incredibly excited to finally be over 21 for my favorite holiday of the year. Lola and I started Friday night with some Jägermeister shots. I told her all about the Tinder guy and she was not as excited about him as I was. She said:

"Martyna, you're going to find a reason not to like him anyway. You always do. He might be perfect and you'll still find something wrong with him and break it off."

She was kind of right but I'd never admit that. I just made a face and said I was going to give him a chance even if there was something very wrong with him. That was a lie, obviously, but for some reason I had a feeling I was going to like that guy.

At the same time, I was freaking out, afraid that I was getting my hopes up. What if he was going to turn out to be a complete weirdo? Or even worse, he'd be short...

We went out to a gross club for underage kids since Lola was still only 20 and our options were quite limited. Somehow, we still ended up dancing on the tables of a creperie in downtown DC. I was a... sexy deer, I guess? Lola was a slutty pumpkin from 'How I Met Your Mother'. It was surely an interesting costume - especially when I was explaining it to my host family when she came over.

The next day we woke up after a night of partying and decided to skip the hangover and go back straight to drinking. We got some bread and made some mimosas; eating bread and dipping it in butter while watching romantic comedies (or 'Grey's Anatomy') was our tradition.

By the time Lola left I was a bit tipsy and didn't really stop drinking until I got into another costume and headed to meet up with my other friends. Unlike Lola, they were actually able to get into proper bars. That night I was dressed up as a princess. I was hoping to meet up with the Tinder guy in one of the bars at Dupont Circle but once again, he said he couldn't come. It was a huge disappointment and I knew if he didn't show up soon, I'd get tired of texting a stranger.

Around 10 PM I was bored, and despite all the crazy amount of alcohol I had that night, I didn't feel drunk at all. I kept texting the guy just because I had lost my party mood and wanted to get out of there. I was constantly hinting at him to come over but he was very slow to get the suggestion. Finally, he texted:

"If I leave now I won't be there till midnight or later…"

"It's fine, I can wait. I've got nothing better to do anyway"

I mean, it was a bit desperate but whatever! I had to know… I just needed to know if this could work out or not. I hated the idea that I was falling for someone I never met and it all could end up being a big waste of my time. I just wanted to get that meeting over with. I had nothing to lose.

I waited for about two hours (parking took him forever) until he finally texted me that he'd be there in five minutes. I walked out of the Public bar and waited in the cold. Dressed up as a princess in my long pink summer dress, black boots, and a tiara. I was freaking out.

Some people were trying to talk to me about my costume and I was way too nervously excited to explain to them that it was not supposed to be scary. I just wanted to be a princess.

Then I saw him walking in between people trying to make his way towards me. My heart stopped... and the rest was history.

Make Me Feel Like a Virgin

I honestly think that you can tell a lot about a relationship by looking back at the first date. At least that's how I feel about ours. There was nothing usual about that very first night. For God's sake, we started our date after midnight. But it will always be one of the best nights of my life.

When I saw Andrew coming up to me he was wearing a red and navy flannel shirt and blue jeans. He looked great. I had no idea why someone that hot would ever be interested in someone like me, but I knew I wanted to get to know him.

We went back to the bar where I had left my friends, got some drinks, and started dancing. By that time I had already had about 15 drinks within the last 24 hours! So yes, I was having a great time dancing over there with the Tinder guy I had just met. He was kind of surprised by how it all started. We went from not knowing each other to dancing and making out on the dancefloor within about five minutes. He was definitely not drunk enough (or at all) to be comfortable with all of that, but I didn't really notice it. 15 drinks would do that to you.

The kiss… It felt good but honestly, I don't remember the details. I don't think I have to explain why. The whole dancing and kissing was so amazing that I got completely lost in it. Andrew didn't seem to feel the same way because at some point he asked if we could change the scenery. So we headed out.

Since DC was my city, I was in charge of our itinerary. No pressure, right? I wanted to show him all the local gems but also, I was a sucker for all the touristy places. Since it was after midnight, most of the best spots were closed so I had to choose between looking like a party girl with some minor alcohol issues or a nerd who loved walking around and looking at old monuments.

I took him to Crepeaway.

Crepeaway was a crazy place. It was a casual creperie during the day, and for whatever reason, they turned their tables into a dancing floor on weekend nights. If you were going to Crepeaway on a Friday or Saturday night, you were probably going to end up dancing on a table. That's just a fact. They didn't sell alcohol though, so it was more of an afterparty spot. Usually by the time people got there, they were already pretty drunk.

We ordered some crepes, sat down, and realized that finally, it was time to start talking. It wasn't that bad though, pretty good actually. Still, we didn't dance. Which was really weird for me considering the fact that only the previous night Lola and I were the first ones to go up on the tables. However, I decided I had freaked him out enough already. I told the dancing beast inside my head to calm down, keep my body still, and focus on the conversation. It wasn't easy but I succeeded.

After a while, we left Crepeaway and faced that awkward moment. It was around 2 AM and most of the places were closing, but we didn't really want to finish our date. It had basically only started.

So what could a girl do in this situation? I took him to the Mall. And since we were in DC, I meant the National Mall - basically a huge piece of grass with some monuments in between and museums on the sides. This was about to be either the most fun or the most boring date ever.

We started walking around and talking a lot. I told him all of my and Lola's stories. How she swam in that basin, how we loved doing after-parties and dancing at the Lincoln Memorial…

Surprisingly, we had a lot of fun just goofing around and walking from monument to monument. I was freezing but I didn't care. I didn't want that night to end.

We got to the World War II Memorial and found the Virginia state column. I took some pictures for him since he was from Virginia, and it was a tradition for everyone to take a picture with their state. We went up the stairs overlooking the memorial and stood there in silence. Then Andrew said:

"You know… I never kissed a girl at the World War II Memorial." - he said.

"Oh, yeah…?" - I replied and waited.

Then waited a bit longer, and then another 10 seconds. He did nothing. Seriously, completely nothing. He just stood there, about five feet away from me, in very awkward silence. Possibly waiting for my move.

There was only one issue. The alcohol had officially left my system, so I was not as bold as I was at the club. Unfortunately, I came back to my boring old-fashioned self who believed that the guy needed to make all the first moves. So I just smiled and walked away.

I was laughing so hard on the inside because the situation was so awkward, but at the same time, I didn't know what else to do. He could've kissed me but he didn't. That was on him…

Anyway, it was a bit weird (meaning it was the most awkward moment in the history of first dates) but we continued like nothing ever happened.

We went back to the fountain area and Andrew mentioned he was curious about how cold the water was. I took it as a challenge to check it out. I took my boots off and before I knew it, we were both doing a lap in the freezing cold water; screaming in misery and laughing at our stupidity at the same time. It was possibly slightly illegal, as all the signs said walking in the fountain was forbidden. Spoiler alert, we both got sick the following week. Also, let's not forget that I was still wearing a sleeveless princess summer dress that gave me literally zero protection from the cold. Plus, high-heeled booties that had stopped being comfortable around midnight.

Shaking from the cold, we ran back to his car and realized that somehow it was already after 5:30 AM. Again, neither of us wanted the night to come to an end. We checked that there was a Starbucks close by that was opening at 6 AM so we headed there to warm up and get some morning coffee (or tea, since to me, coffee is the worst drink that was ever invented).

The Starbucks people were late so we had to wait for about 20 minutes, still freezing in the cold October morning weather. Andrew had already given me his jacket a while ago. Of course, I was still freezing, but tried to act all tough and not give it away. He was smarter than that. He came up to me, hugged my shivering body, and kept me in his arms, giving me some of his warmth.

He didn't know it back then but this was the most intimate I'd ever felt with a guy. I was not a hugger. I had never been a touchy-feely person who would hug random people just because it was nice to meet them. I actually avoided hugging people by quickly pulling out my hand before they got too close. I didn't even hug my parents! I didn't like touching people at all… Besides Lola… I was always all over her.

But with Drew… I stayed in his arms and kind of enjoyed it. This was huge. He held me and I didn't want to run away. It almost seemed like that was the moment my body and mind decided that he was the one.

Of course, I didn't say anything. I was just standing there, not knowing what to do with my arms or my hands or my whole body, yet still appreciating his warmth. Just another very awkward situation that I'll never forget. On the inside, though? It was a breakthrough…

We finally got inside the Starbucks and sat down with some coffee and tea. At that moment our date officially became an all-nighter. We both didn't seem to mind. Instead, we started playing 20 Questions. Question for question, answer for answer. He got all the answers right. I liked him more with every single sentence and I had no idea what to do about that. I couldn't stop thinking:

"Why the hell is he interested in me???"

After another hour of talking, we decided it was time to go home. We got into his car and he dropped me off at my host family's house. He didn't kiss me goodbye, though, which was kind of disappointing. But at the same time, my host dad was outside walking the dogs when I was getting out of the car, so maybe he was just feeling awkward. I hoped it wasn't a pattern with us.

Trying to keep it low-key was not an option. It was 8 AM and I was getting out of a guy's car, still wearing my princess dress and a tiara. I braced myself to answer my host family's burning questions. Right before getting to the door, I turned around, smiled at Drew, and walked into the house - trying to pretend like my life hadn't just been turned upside down.

Who Friendzoned Who?

We went on one more date before I headed to New York for a marathon. I really enjoyed it and had a great time with him, but he still didn't kiss me. Well, besides that one time in the club when I basically drunkenly forced myself onto him. I started thinking that he might not be interested in me after all. Maybe he just wanted to be friends? But then would he text me all day every day and want to meet again if that's all it was? I was confused.

I couldn't do anything about it though since I had a marathon to run. I went to New York for the weekend and I was supposed to run on Sunday. I walked around the city with Lola and we met up with my Polish friend Susana. Both of them were volunteering at the marathon to support me, and I was super excited to have them as my own personal cheer-squad.

Susana was always there for me. We were friends from childhood, and honestly, for a very long time, we didn't keep in touch besides on some random occasions. But we had a lot in common - we both were obsessed with traveling. And when I say obsessed, I mean obsessed. Susana was the only friend who changed her postcode (or country) as often as I did. We connected together again during our senior year of high school when she joined my drama club and we had been best friends ever since. She was that kind of friend who I could not talk to for months and then pick up right where we left off. She was always way busier than I was and I loved that about her. She was also one of the most genuine souls I'd ever met. I felt privileged to call her my friend. When she told me she was going to the US at the same time that I was planning on coming back as an au pair, we knew it was destiny. We made sure to meet up as often as possible, even if she lived in Colorado and I lived in DC. And she still made it to New York. Not many people would schedule everything around a marathon they didn't even run, just to be there for their friends.

The night before the race we went to Dumbo and sat down at the riverfront. After a whole day of walking around the Big Apple, I was exhausted and couldn't wait to get to bed. Also… I couldn't stop thinking about the Tinder guy. He was amazing. I was so into him... I felt like he knew that but for some reason, he wasn't making any moves.

I was staring at Brooklyn Bridge that night thinking about all of our conversations about New York. He had never been to the city and really wanted to visit it. It was so weird to me that even though he lived so close to New York he had never experienced its beauty. I couldn't stop the feeling that next time I really wanted to bring him with me. I wanted to show him everything I had seen so far. Honestly, I wanted to show him the whole world. It was the weirdest feeling I had ever experienced.

I didn't know what to do with it. But I did know that I definitely didn't want to be just friends with Andrew.

*****

The next day, I ran the New York City Marathon. It was an absolutely life-changing experience. That crowd - people cheering me on and trying to help me get through every single mile. I loved every minute of it.

At mile 23, Susana joined me for the last stretch. As soon as she saw me, she ran up to me all smiley and super happy. Since it was a water station, she instantly face-planted herself into the ground whilst still holding up her phone. She got up quickly and kept on recording the video for friends and family. At that moment, I hated her so badly. She was way too happy while I was struggling with every step. I loved her for it but I also wanted to punch her in that cheerful face. She kept saying:

"You can do it"- and I just wanted to scream…

"I CAN'T!"

The best part of it all was that I ran the whole damn thing. Didn't walk even for a moment (well, just to get some water). I finished the marathon in 5 hours and 19 minutes. Maybe for some people it's not a great time but that day I was beyond proud of myself for even finishing it. It was by far one of the greatest accomplishments of my life.

Although, maybe the best part was when Lola pretended that I was a heart transplant survivor just so she could see me at the finish line. Since the NYC marathon was security-heavy, Susana couldn't run with me all the way to the end. Lola took matters into her own hands and convinced the security that we had flown all the way from Europe the night before just so I could run a marathon after my heart transplant. Apparently I was dying and me running the whole thing was a miracle. If you asked me, that wasn't that far from the truth. At mile 26, I really was dying.

Unfortunately, Lola's plan failed. She couldn't find me and I got lost after crossing the finish line. I don't know why the race organizers thought it was a good idea to make us walk another mile or so before we could meet our friends and families but by the time I got to the crowd awaiting the runners, Lola and Susana were absolutely terrified. I guess running without a phone wasn't such a great idea.

It got dark very quickly as it was November in New York, and we were almost late for the bus taking us back to DC. Lola had another genius idea of calling my name through the speaker but

I was so exhausted, cold and out of it that I didn't even realize I was being called up, multiple times. Finally, we all found each other and ran (yes, RAN) to the bus station. We said our goodbyes to Susana and headed back home.

We had to change buses in Baltimore. By then it had been about five or six hours since I had finished the race and I still hadn't even had an opportunity to take a shower or EAT. I begged Lola to get an Uber back to DC since I lived on the Maryland side of the city, closer to Baltimore. I said I'd pay for her Uber to Virginia. But Lola, cheap Spanish Lola, refused my poor exhausted body the rest it needed. She decided it was only reasonable to wait for the bus.

If you're wondering why we thought it was a good idea to take a bus right after running a marathon… I had to work the next day. Per usual, I didn't want to use my priceless vacation days and apparently running a marathon was not an excuse to get any special treatment from my host family.

In the end, I survived. We got back to DC, ordered Ubers to our homes and the next week, I went for a 13-mile run just for fun. I'm not sure why.

*****

When I came back to DC, I was over the moon to see Andrew again. The next few weeks were great. I kept on hanging out with him and I loved every single date… but then, was it even a date? He still hadn't kissed me and I started losing hope. He was way too hot for me to be just friends with him. However, I'd rather die than make the first move. As any reasonable girl would.

After our third date, he dropped me off at the house again. I felt like he was going for a kiss but then I went for a hug. The whole thing turned out to be kind of awkward. I walked into my room, completely defeated. Clementine was obviously waiting for me on my bed, very happy that I came back to her. I looked at her and dramatically said:

"Clem, I think he just doesn't like me. Did he just friendzone me???"

Clem looked at me and wiggled her tail. My phone vibrated.

"If I don't kiss you next time I see you, I'll go crazy," said the text.

I'm not lying. It sounds cheesy and way too movie-like but that's exactly what happened.

I smiled and did a little dance.

"He likes me! Clem, he really likes me!" - I started screaming and jumping around. Clem clearly had no idea why I was so excited but she was happy for me as always.

"You better do it next time you have a chance," I replied. I was cool. I was chill. I couldn't care less if he kissed me. I was in charge…

God, we were acting like teenagers! Trying to figure out if we liked or liked LIKED each other. It was silly but kind of magical.

Later on, I found out that he felt the same way about me. Meaning he thought I didn't like LIKE him and he didn't want to push. It's insane to think that we both started off thinking there was no chemistry between us. At the same time, it felt like that's exactly what I needed to fall in love with him. Time and patience. No one else ever gave me that before.

Never Been Kissed

I'll always remember our fourth date for a few reasons. Firstly, I was freezing as hell. Well, I was freezing as hell throughout the first few months of us dating, since we started going out in late October. We spent 90% of the time in his car on heated seats with hot air blowing into our faces. This date was no different.

Secondly, I ate Hibachi for the first time in my life.

Thirdly, I was wearing heels and was super uncomfortable, while walking in the woods for no reason.

Fourthly, the guy of my dreams finally kissed me for the second time and this time I was sober enough to fully remember it.

Right after we ate dinner, Andrew asked me if I was up for an adventure. And of course, I was. He took me somewhere near his work. At least that's what he said. To me it was a random dark wooded path. We got out of the car, freezing air pinching our cheeks, and walked towards the sketchy-looking woods.

As usual in winter, I was in high-heeled booties. I was trying to be brave and not to complain but the truth was, I could barely walk. With all the rocks and sand and mud, it was a real struggle. But I kept going. With a Tinder guy who technically I barely knew. In the dark and quiet woods. Having no idea where we were. Freezing my fingers off. I started reconsidering my idea of an "adventure".

We finally got to this little lake (more like a pond) overlooking some residential neighborhood on one side and a highway on the other. It was nice and quiet. We stood in the darkness not talking that much and just appreciating the view of the dark sky above us. Andrew hugged me, opening his jacket. I sneaked my body inside and enjoyed his warmth. It was the perfect moment for a kiss, but then again, we'd had loads of those and he seemed to never take the hint.

But this time was different. No stupid lines like "I've never kissed a girl next to this lake before" or anything like that. He just leaned down and kissed me.

That was honestly one of the best kisses of my life. And oh boy, it was long. It was magical. With the freezing air around us, stars shining over our heads and the sound of passing cars in the background.

If you ask me, that was our first kiss. Screw drunk make-out sessions in bars. This is how every first kiss should look like. A lot of moments with Andrew would follow the footsteps of that one perfect kiss. For such a spontaneous guy, Andrew had a great ability for choosing the ideal moments, ideal locations, and ideal ways to do everything that mattered.

*****

That November was possibly one of the best months of my life. Well, the first year of dating Andrew was in general, the best year of my life. His 24th birthday was only a month after we met. I got us Wizards tickets. They were pretty good, but about three hours before the game my host mom asked me if I wanted courtside tickets from her friend. I almost lost it and I knew Andrew would too. I mean, courtside tickets. I was about to win the 'girlfriend of the year' award and technically I wasn't even his girlfriend… yet. He was about an hour late, of course. I knew he had to work but c'mon! Finally, after about an hour of parking issues, he got to the arena. He had no idea about the courtside seats. And I said absolutely nothing, while leading him to the third row and handing him a plastic ticket.

"Happy early birthday," I said.

He couldn't believe these were our seats. And that we were allowed to have any food and alcohol we wanted. He wasn't like me, I'd be jumping and screaming while he seemed only mildly excited. But I knew it was a once in a lifetime experience for him and for whatever reason I wanted to give it all to him.

For his actual birthday I struggled. What do you get for a guy you've known less than a month? I was sure we were more than friends but technically we weren't even in a relationship yet. I wanted to make his first birthday with me special, but without giving crazy clingy vibes.

We ordered pizza and I put 24 candles in it. I made his roommate sing "Happy Birthday" with me and then Andrew blew his candles. I made sure he made a wish.

I got him Christmas lights for his new apartment and a framed photo of us from that Wizards game. I knew that move was risky. I couldn't decide whether I was being cute or way too much. Probably both. Giving him a framed photo of us that early on was kind of a stretch but it didn't seem to scare him off. He put it on his dresser and hung up the lights. He had just moved out of his parents' and I was excited to be a part of it all.

*****

After the marathon Andrew was really impressed with me, so in December he agreed to run a race together. I chose a Jingle Run organized by one of DC's running groups. A 15k run in Christmas sweaters, it was supposed to be fun and easy. I got us our race packets the day before and told Andrew to meet up with me at the Lincoln Memorial steps for the sunrise.

I always loved that sunrise view and I was hoping to share it with Andrew. I didn't really mean it in a romantic way, I got all of my friends to see it with me just as a fun and unusual thing to do in DC.

Unsurprisingly, Steven, Andrew's roommate, wasn't happy with everything that was happening. He had expected to move in with Andrew and have the best bachelor year of their lives. He was hoping to be scoring a different girl every weekend. Meanwhile Andrew was leaving the house at 7 AM on a Sunday morning to watch the sunrise and run a 15k with a Tinder chick.

According to Steven, the framed picture, the sunrise… All of these were typical practices of desperate girls trying to trick guys like Andrew into falling in love with them. Well, falling in love with me. But despite Steven's opinion, I wasn't that smart. All the cliche moves both Andrew and I were making came weirdly naturally to us. We weren't trying to fall in love with each other. No one tricked anyone. We just couldn't help becoming a cliche. Whatever, Steven...

Meanwhile, I was waiting for Andrew at the Lincoln Memorial. He was late, of course. One thing I learned very quickly about him… punctuality was not his strong suit.

He almost missed the sunrise. Once he finally showed up, we enjoyed the view for about five minutes before we both admitted it was way too cold to sit on the concrete stairs. We ran back to his car and headed straight to Starbucks for hot cocoa. Then again, we ran to the start line. Well, to be clear… I was freaking out that we would be late and I kind of made him run to the start line. By the time we got there (with plenty of time to spare) we had probably run over a mile or two already. Let's say, Andrew wasn't exactly thrilled with me.

We had an agreement that we were running separately. I was sure Andrew was going to be much faster than me, and of course, he was. I had never had anyone to do something like that with me before. It was fun to do it together even if technically we didn't run together. I knew Andrew was somewhere there, kicking my ass and I liked it. It motivated me.

Afterward, we went back to my host family's house, took a shower, and walked down the street for brunch. It was nice to have Andrew in my area for once and I loved hanging out with him. I was also freaking out because I had no idea what we were. People called him my boyfriend quite often, and every single time, I only mumbled back:

"He's not my boyfriend."

We hung out for the rest of the day and ended up grabbing dinner in Shake Shack, which was my favorite fast food place in the US because of their vegetarian Shroom Burgers.

We were eating our fries and I even got a REAL burger. That was so unusual for me, but I guess I wanted to impress him by eating meat. Can't blame a girl for trying. In the end I ate the bun, the toppings and took a small bite of my patty. Once again, I realized I still didn't like meat. We were having so much fun and laughing out loud… when out of nowhere Andrew asked THAT question:

"So… how would you describe me to people? Do you say that I'm your boyfriend?"

Instantly, I felt my face going full-on red. I was so embarrassed. He made me feel like I was back in elementary school and was trying to give a Valentine's Day card to a boy I liked. After a long pause, I started the confusing explanation. I told him how I hadn't thought of him as my boyfriend, but I liked him more than a friend. I was so in my head, it took me forever to come up with an explanation without using the words "boyfriend", "exclusive", or "relationship".

For me, it was definitely the most awkward conversation in the history of "checking the relationship's status" conversations ever. But again, that seemed quite on brand for us. We had a talent for making everything extremely awkward and difficult. It took us about an hour to decide that we were not going to see other people. Not that we were beforehand… With all that time we spent texting and hanging out with each other, we had no time left for the other people. But according to modern dating rules, we had to agree on not hooking up with others.

When I finally thought we had everything figured out and I was driving Drew back to his car, he blew out:

"Wait, I'm confused. Are we a couple or not?!"

"I don't know..." I said.

Why? Why the hell were we so awkward?!

"Don't make me say it..."

"Say what?" I asked.

At this point, I was just mean... or childish. I could've easily cut his misery short and told him that we were a couple. Yet for some lame reason - probably connected to the fact that he was about to be my very first grown-up boyfriend - I wanted to make sure he said those words so I would have had no doubts about what we were.

"I feel like I'm back in high school," he said. I wouldn't have known, boys in high school just wanted to sleep with me, not date me. Another long pause... "Martyna, will you be my girlfriend?"

Now it was my turn for yet another long pause. I wasn't trying to be dramatic or anything like that. I sincerely couldn't speak. Finally, I managed to choke out:

"Yes!"

I still remember that "yes". It was terrible. My voice cracked about 10 times in that one tiny little word. It was a very high-pitched "yes" that to me, sounded like nails on a chalkboard. But hey, I said it. It was done. I officially had a boyfriend!

Steven & My Friends

There's nothing like the time when a couple decides to let their friends start meeting each other…

My personal favorite was always Steven, Andrew's roommate. Steven was a typical American jock. He was handsome enough to get some girls interested in him but not smart enough to do anything about it. He was a huge stoner. He made me realize some people considered weed as an everyday thing. And that basically changed my innocent and naive approach to drugs forever. Before meeting Steven, I thought only idiots and criminals would go to work or even drive after smoking. He taught me that many Americans did that. I was shocked, but thanks to Lola's influence I was better prepared for it than I would have been a few months before.

Not only did Steven illegally consume drugs like I consume candy, he was also a completely oblivious jerk to a lot of girls. Still, I grew to love him like a brother I never had. Well, besides the one I had in Poland who used to beat me up when I was a child…

Steven became a huge part of my life. I baked for him, screamed at him when I thought he was being an asshole to other girls, and encouraged him to score all the time. Andrew and I went on numerous double dates with him... well, more like five, but all with different girls. We also took him out to bars. Andrew would be his wingman and I would be drinking, just entertained by the whole situation.

One day we tried to introduce him to Lola. It didn't work out that well. We went to a secret concert and it turned out to be a cute winery. As soon as I saw Steven in his sweatpants, I knew that night wasn't going to be the start of a beautiful relationship between our best friends, as I had hoped it might be. I ordered a bottle of wine, then another one. By the end of the evening, they still hadn't had a single conversation with each other. Meanwhile, I was tipsy as hell after drinking almost two bottles of wine on my own.

A few more times I tried to convince them it was a great idea to hang out together. Unfortunately, no one seemed interested in fulfilling my dreams of double dating with my best friend. Later on, Steven turned out to be into a different friend of mine, Aroa.

Aroa was beautiful, amazing, and super hot. She was smart and her English was great for an au pair. She was the one who I last-minute invited to my birthday trip to Nashville. We became great friends and kept hanging out together afterwards. Honestly... I never saw her as that hot chick guys would fall for. She was always my friend who was too lazy to go to the gym and had tacos and fried oreos with me for brunch every Sunday.

Clearly, I was the only one who saw her that way. She always had a bunch of guys in love with her, ready to pay for her drinks and invite her to the most exclusive parties. She was also very picky but it worked in her favor as she always ended up hooking up with hot or famous guys.

After the Lola fiasco, we introduced Steven to Aroa. We all went out dancing and he had all night to make a move. Surprise, he did nothing... again! I spent all night dancing with Andrew (grinding on his crotch) while Steven was completely on his own with Aroa. It was beyond my understanding how he didn't do anything about it.

He was so into her. He wouldn't stop talking about her for months after that night. We gave him many, I mean MANY, opportunities to make a move but at some point it was clear it would never happen.

For New Year's Eve, Lola and I threw a tiny rager. We had about 8 single girls waiting for cute guys to talk to them… and Steven left to meet up with some Tinder girl downtown. Unsurprisingly, nothing happened with that one either. At some point, I just gave up on Steven and had to acknowledge he was a lost cause.

From then on, I promised myself not to ever try to hook him up with any of my friends again. Still, Andrew and I never failed to support him in his attempts!

The Best Time of the Year!

Christmas time was always my favorite of all. It was the time of the year when I dropped everything and started baking! And that year, I finally had a boyfriend to fit into my stereotypical Hallmark Christmas fantasies.

It was Christmas Eve and everyone was excited. On Christmas Day, I was supposed to go to Drew's house to meet his family for the very first time. So, my host mom decided that we'd have a Christmas Eve dinner together, just like in Polish tradition where the most important day for us was the 24th.

I was very excited to spend yet another Christmas in the States. Of course, I was trying to make sure everything was perfect. I cooked Pierogi, which was a traditional Polish meal - kind of like dumplings, just bigger and better. I baked loads of pies and cakes and cookies. Kirsten asked me to help out with the family dinner, so at around 3 PM I started preparing everything.

Unfortunately, she was drunk by 4 PM. I was finishing up dinner when she came downstairs and started blaming everyone for not wanting to hang out with her. She kept on repeating it was the worst Christmas of her life and that no one cared about her. Finally, she said the dinner was canceled and everyone should just go to their rooms.

The kids were crying and begging her to stop saying those things. I kept my head down trying to ignore her, hoping she'd calm down and we could proceed to having a civilized dinner together. As usual, my host dad told her she was being ridiculous and ordered her to take a nap or watch TV before dinner.

Finally, we sat down to eat what I prepared. Everyone thanked me for cooking but my host kids obviously hated the food. Kirsten started getting annoyed again. She complained that I was the only one looking nice - while she was in sweatpants and a Patagonia sweatshirt. I couldn't tell if she was mad at me or herself. It almost felt like it was my fault that I'd treated Christmas more special than she had.

When we were done with the meal, my parents called and wanted Kirsten to give me the present they had all prepared for me. Apparently, my big brother had got in touch with her and asked her to get me a brand new Fitbit on their behalf.

Honestly, I was kind of expecting that. It's incredibly hard to surprise me. I pretended to be surprised, though. I was genuinely excited about the new watch. What I wasn't so excited for was drunk Kirsten. I was still in the middle of the conversation with my parents when she started getting into the camera, singing and dancing. My parents didn't know any better. They just thought she was super American, fun and so awesome. For me, it was all an act though. I knew she wasn't like that on a daily basis. She was stiff and rude most of the time, smiling when people were around and talking behind their backs when they walked away.

When she was drunk, she was in a great mood when someone was watching. Just like at the concert. She was dancing and having the time of her life. And just like at the concert, as soon as the conversation ended, her mood changed and again - it was the worst Christmas of her life. Finally, she went to bed.

It wasn't the first and it wouldn't be the last time the whole family had to deal with Kirsten's drunken mood swings. Ever since the kids came back from the camp back in July, Kirsten would go up to her room straight after work and fall asleep at 5 PM. We were lucky if she didn't wake up a few hours later just so she could fight with her husband, or scream at the children.

She never screamed at me though. She was just awfully nice, pretending that I couldn't see that there was something wrong with her… or with that family.

It was a really terrible Christmas Eve. Probably the worst of my life. All of that after I spent weeks helping my host dad to get the perfect presents for her. Just because I didn't want to hear more complaints about how no one cared about her. Well, I guess I shouldn't have been surprised that nothing we ever did was enough for her.

I know she was depressed at that moment. I could see it in her eyes and her face, which seemed to be getting 10 years older every single time she drank. I felt really bad for her. I waited for my host dad to wake up and take her to rehab or try to help her in any way. I even talked to him about it but he just kept repeating:

"I know Kirsten has an issue but we can only try to be nice to her and not to set her off."

That was his reasoning for everything she did, and afterward, the subject was over. Fortunately, they were leaving the next day for a ski trip so I couldn't wait to get some rest and finally be drama-free for a week or so. Also, my friend Gina was coming over from England to spend New Year's Eve with me, so that was definitely something to look forward to.

*****

Christmas Day was stressful in a completely different way. I was anxious about meeting Andrew's family. From what I had heard, all of his mom's side was supposed to be there. I wore a nice red dress that was not too short, but still decided to go with thick black tights underneath to make it even more proper. I was freaking out!

I made this huge gift basket for them with Polish candy and snacks from a Polish store that I spent a fortune on. I was pretty sure I overdid it but still was slightly scared I didn't do enough. Also, I brought loads of Pierogi and a baked cheesecake... Yeah, I definitely overdid it.

It turned out Andrew's family was great and they really liked me - at least I had a feeling they did. They had this crazy tradition that everyone had to open their presents in front of others and comment on every single one of them. That went on for hours! It was really entertaining, though. Kind of embarrassing when everyone was staring at me and waiting for my reaction to the presents I completely didn't expect to get… but still fun. I definitely felt like a part of the family and it was a great feeling.

Also, I met Andrew's best friend, Justin. He was … well, he was something. I'm not sure how I should exactly describe Justin. A male version of Lola, perhaps. But gross and even more inappropriate. Maybe a little bit less crazy, but more vulgar. They definitely had one thing in common, though. People either loved or hated them.

After spending all day with Andrew's family, we came back to his townhouse in Alexandria and spent the night together, just the two of us.. We had some wine and ate some more food. We watched a movie and I passed out halfway through.

That was one of my favorite Christmas Days of my life. The year before, I went to Bali - so believe me, the bar was high. However, somehow, just a month into dating, Andrew made me feel like a part of his family. That was a first for me… and I liked it.

The next day I came back home and said goodbye to my host family as they went to the airport to catch a plane to Aspen.

I felt a huge relief when they left. I realized I didn't enjoy spending time with them anymore. It wasn't only their fault; for the first time, I had my own life in the US that was completely separate from theirs. Still, they were definitely the main reason why I didn't feel like they were my home anymore. I used to consider them my home away from home, but then I found amazing friends and Andrew, and even his family. Every one of them treated me so kindly and appreciated me… while my host family couldn't even get their shit together for one night that they knew was very important to me. Instead, they just focused on their family drama, and I simply didn't want to be a part of it.

*****

One of my favorite dates with Andrew was in Annapolis right before New Year's Eve. I was falling in love hard. Especially that day.

Annapolis was a small town about 45 minutes away from my host family's house. I used to drive my host kids there for a sailing camp, and I loved its charm and old-school buildings. With its colorful little houses and brick-covered streets, Annapolis looked like a typical small town from an American movie. The Chesapeake Bay, where it was located, was one of the most popular fishing spots in that region. Annapolis was famous for being a boating paradise… Or whatever you call a place where rich DC people hang out on their yachts. It was hard to be judgemental, though, when my host family had a membership at the Annapolis Yacht Club and I absolutely loved that place.

Since Andrew had never been to that area before, I was excited about our date. I wanted to take him to one of my favorite ice cream shops and to get some cream of crab with french fries. That was literally the only purpose of our little trip.

It was a December afternoon when he picked me up from my host family's house and we drove down to Maryland. It was really warm for that time of the year. I was only wearing jeans and a shirt while enjoying the gloomy weather. I loved the mist covering our bodies and the dark clouds above our heads.

We started off by parking Andrew's car by Annapolis Naval Academy and walked towards the main street. I always loved that view. The street was situated on a hill, and while going up you could see different local stores and gift shops on both sides, and a big church at the top. It looked really cool, with big dark clouds surrounding it.

I knew Andrew was collecting stickers for his guitar case so I took him to the gift shop with me and bought him an Annapolis sticker as a souvenir, when he wasn't looking. Then we walked to my favorite bar and got some seafood and my old-time favorite - cream of crab with fries.

We found this little bookshop far away from the main street. We went in and looked around for a long time, trying to find some interesting books. Andrew was always interested in astrology, zodiac signs, etc. so he grabbed an astrology book, sat down in a comfy armchair, and started reading it. I sat down on one side of the chair and let him read some crazy things about Libras - my zodiac sign. Again, I bought him the book when he wasn't looking and planned on giving it to him with the sticker later on.

There was nothing special about that date. There was still a Christmas feel to it and I was there with him. And that was more than enough. Somehow, Andrew was always able to make me feel like we were in a movie. Every step, every smile, dancing on the street under Christmas lights... Everything seemed to be surreal.

It started getting late so we went back to the car and headed back to DC. Andrew dropped me off at my house and I was not prepared to feel the way I did. I knew he had promised Steven to hang out with him that night, but I wished he stayed. And yes, a huge part of me was just petrified of being alone in that huge house. But there was also another part of me...

A part that was starting to realize that, after not even two months, I was starting to get attached. I wanted to spend all of my time with him. I wanted him to sleep over as much as he could. I wanted to have him all to myself.

I also knew that all of this was way too fresh and new to have these kinds of expectations or feelings! But at the same time, I just couldn't get enough of him.

Still, I kept on telling everyone that he was too hot for me and was probably gonna break up with me any minute. I was so freaked out by that possibility, and that everyone would laugh at me for being lame and falling in love with someone that was not that into me. So, I just preferred to give a heads-up to anyone who'd ask about my new (first) relationship. It was weird and I knew it. I just couldn't help but feel like all of this was too good to be true.

*****

Finally, we got to New Year's Eve. There were a lot of things going on at that time. I was stressed out because of my host family, I was still discovering what it meant for me to be in a relationship, and I started realizing I was falling for a guy I barely knew. The last one was probably the main reason for my stupid and immature behavior at Lola's party.

For months we had been trying to figure out what to do that night. Then we found out that Lola's host family would be away for the whole Christmas break, so we decided to have a party at their house. It wasn't the most responsible choice but it was also not the most irresponsible thing we did that year. We tried to keep it low-key and put everyone in the basement. Lola walked around party-proofing everything. We did our best not to invite too many people. And we kind of succeeded… Well, if we don't mention our German friend Diana and Andrew's friend Patrick hooking up in Lola's bedroom - making her sleep on the couch and listen to everyone having sex. But that's not important. The important thing was that everyone had fun and we didn't do anything that would get Lola kicked out of the program.

It was a crazy time for us since we both had some people visiting. There was Gina who I met in Canada back in July and there was Laura who, for some reason, was Lola's friend.

Why "for some reason"? Because she couldn't be further from what Lola and I stood for. And what we stood for was crazy and unforgettable fun, skinny dipping, getting drunk and making out with boys we didn't even like… you get the gist. Meanwhile,

Laura seemed to be constantly unhappy with everything we were doing. She kept calling her mom who was back in Spain - always ready to jump on a plane if she found out Laura did something against God's will. I wish I was exaggerating.

That day I had to work in the morning. Even though my host mom was just hanging out at the house and had nothing better to do than to sit and watch TV. There's no rest for the au pair kind...

As soon as I was done, I packed the car up with the craziest things you could ever come up with (including some pots and pans I borrowed when my host mom wasn't watching). We ran up to the store to get the largest amount of alcohol I had ever gotten, before finally driving to Lola's house. Since she was off the whole week, she had plenty of time to clean up and get the house party-proofed, make an enormous pot of Sangria, and in the end, cook plenty of Spanish food that would last us for days. I loved how seriously she treated her job as a party hostess. I was the same way, so no wonder we were such a great couple… I meant friends! I said friends, right?

By the time Andrew and Steven arrived at the party, I was already quite tipsy. Since Andrew was always late, we kind of developed a routine. I'd start off by waiting for him, patiently. Then I'd slowly start getting annoyed. This would lead me to putting way too much wine in my system, which would conclude in me being super excited to see him when he finally arrived. In the end, everyone was happy.

Per usual, I had a great idea that night. A very immature, cheesy, possibly high-school-level idea. But at the same time - a pretty fun one. I made a bet with Drew. We were not allowed to touch or kiss each other for the whole night. There was no prize, I just wanted to prove he'd break first. Which would also prove he was really into me and at the end of the day, that's all I wanted. I just needed the validation that he couldn't resist me. He was sure that he could, though, and that I'd be the one losing. That's how one of the sexiest nights of our relationship began.

We were both very competitive and committed to making it very difficult for each other. Not long after he arrived, we started bending the rules. We decided touching was okay as long as we didn't kiss. Of course, I was desperate for the win so I played dirty. I was wearing a black mini-dress with a deep V-neck which barely covered anything. I had a black push up bra that had two strings with tiny silver beads on them, crossing over my boobs - perfectly complementing the V-neck. I even had some make-up on!

All the tension was amazing, and the teasing was way too fun. After possibly half a pot of Sangria some things started getting blurry. It almost felt like my brain stopped registering and I became my feelings. All I could do was feel the sparks flying between me and Andrew.

Somehow we ended up in a bathroom together, and I was so sure he was going to break at that moment. He almost did. I was sitting on the sink with my legs wrapped around his waist. My dress was tucked all the way up. I knew he could see my stockings showing off a bit of bare skin right before my underwear line started. I had never felt so sexy before. We stared into each other's eyes for a couple of minutes. He almost kissed me… and then he left the bathroom.

Maybe this whole bet was silly and immature but at the same time it was possibly the best pre-game of all times. I loved every minute of it and I didn't care how silly it seemed from the outside.

It took a lot from me not to lose that bet. I was drunk and horny. I was on the verge of losing, so I had to take a break from Drew. That's why I switched to Lola. It was kind of a loophole in Andrew's and I's relationship. He was allowed to hang out with other people at parties as long as I was allowed to get flirty with my best friend. In my 22-year-old mind it made perfect sense.

Sometime after midnight, I was sitting on the couch, just staring at the wall for no reason - possibly more drunk than I'd like to admit. I looked to the side and saw Andrew coming up to me. He charged, grabbed me, and put me back on my feet. He kissed me hard and I got completely lost in it. It was surprising and raw and it took us right to the guest bedroom. We were so turned on we couldn't even bother with taking my dress off.

It was dark, messy, and too blurry for my very tipsy mind to register everything. Once again, I became my feelings and I forgot about the outside world.

We woke up the next morning and it was officially 2019. We hung out in bed for a very long time not ever wanting to leave that bubble we created. Going into a new year with Andrew felt like everything I had ever wished for came true. It was perfect. We were perfect.

Finally, we left the bedroom and faced a very annoyed Lola. I had a feeling she'd never forgive me for the sleepless night we just gave her. Well, and for the fact that multiple people got laid in her house, while she was all alone on the couch.

On my way back to DC, I couldn't stop crying because I was starting to feel the weight of all the decisions I had to make very soon. I knew I wanted to travel the world and then move back to London, but I also couldn't imagine leaving Andrew behind. I didn't want to lose him.

I was a strong believer that the way you spent your January 1st would dictate how the rest of the year would go for you. And that's exactly what happened in 2019 for me. I had the best time of my life. I also spent a lot of it a bit confused, missing Andrew, and crying in the car.

That Taboo Subject

While Lola and I partied our holiday season away, Gina was completely jetlagged and also not used to the craziness of hanging out with the two of us. She missed all of our parties throughout that week. She clearly didn't expect any of that when she agreed to come and visit me. That didn't stop us from having fun though. Just a bit of a different type of fun. More reasonable, with less alcohol involved.

We even went to a basketball game together. We tried to make it a triple date. Me and Andrew, Steven and Gina, plus the two of our friends who hooked up at Lola's party. Of course, Steven couldn't even commit to a casual hangout with a girl. My friend Diana decided that Patrick was just a one night stand and it was on Andrew to let the poor guy know… So we ended up going alone. Which was kind of funny since if you knew Gina, you'd know that an NBA game was the last place you'd expect to see her.

Surprisingly, we had so much fun. The Wizards won that night, which didn't happen that often. It was just us two, having a girls' night at the basketball game. Something we probably never expected to do but somehow it didn't feel weird at all.

We were leaving the Capital One arena when we heard screams

and saw everyone running away from the metro station, pushing us back into the stadium.

I was petrified. I just kept thinking how tiny Gina was and that I couldn't afford to lose her. I knew that she could be easily run over by others so I kept pushing through the crowd while holding her hand and dragging her with me. I wanted to get out of that screaming crowd as soon as possible since we had no idea what was going on. We ran back into the arena and hid at the lower seats level waiting for the madness to be over. Other people had the same idea. We could hear them saying that there was a shooting at the platform where everyone was waiting for a metro back home.

I had never been so scared in my life. We were shocked, and afraid that at any time someone would come in and try to shoot us too. We sat in silence for half an hour, shaking and not saying a word. Finally, it all seemed to be over. We got out of the building just to see the metro being closed down and people slowly coming back to normal. I let my host dad know what was going on and he told us to order an Uber home. Gina was already texting her parents and I felt so bad for putting her in that position.

Still, in silence, we got into the car and let the guy drive us back home. We didn't say a word, and I texted Lola and Andrew. I was so scared and couldn't stop shaking. Silent tears were running down my cheeks and I just couldn't stop thinking:

"Why? Why would anyone do that to other people?"

The next day we were very quiet, just sat on the couch and watched TV in silence. It definitely took us a few days to feel more confident with being outside. At the same time, I realized I had to get used to the fact I lived in a country with a gun violence issue. I mean, I knew that before. But to hear about it and to live through it - that was a completely different story.

I was able to move on and almost forgot about that whole situation. I guess, I had no other choice. The fear never left though. The deep feeling in the back of my mind that I wasn't safe. Wherever I'd go, I would scan people to see if they could be hiding a gun in their hoodie or a bag. It didn't keep me up all night. It didn't stop me from doing things. I just never felt safe again. Sadly, that was the reality of living in the US and somehow, I learned to live with it.

Down South

When Gina left, I was about to run another race - this time in Charleston, SC. I convinced Andrew and Lola to come with me. Well, Steven was supposed to come too but surprise! - he bailed last minute. We rented an amazing Airbnb 30 minutes away from the city and headed there after work on a Friday night. We drove all night, taking turns driving, and got there around 5 AM.

It was super dark and a bit secluded, so we kept on trespassing on different properties while trying to find the Airbnb. It kind of felt like a perfect setting for a horror movie. The kind where everyone gets killed at the end. After about an hour of searching and driving back and forth, we finally found it. It was a beautiful old southern house. Big and only slightly creepy. It had an amazing porch up front and a bunch of bedrooms we didn't need.

Andrew and I had only about 30 minutes to change and head out to the race. When we got there, it was still dark and freaking cold. Somehow, he managed to convince me into getting breakfast at McDonald's. I'd never do that on my own but at the same time I loved how this felt like our little tradition. Meeting before sunrise, getting a crappy breakfast, and then running into the cold. I was okay with that becoming a thing.

The race itself seemed long; at some points the route was quite boring, and the gloomy and cold weather was not making things easier. But we completed yet another race together, and it was actually my best time for a half marathon, so I considered it a success.

When we headed back to the Airbnb, we were exhausted! You know who wasn't, though?

Apparently, Lola. While we were gone, she didn't go to sleep at all. She managed to kayak on the private lake that was attached to our place, and take a romantic bath in candlelight in our bathroom - while being naked for most of it. Of course, she had photos to show me when we got back. The idea of her taking nudes all that time while we were running a half-marathon on no sleep was weirdly not at all surprising.

The rest of the trip was amazing even if very short. We had only a full Saturday (we slept through a big part of it after the race) and a half-Sunday. Yes, it seemed crazy to take a 10-hour drive all the way to South Carolina just to be there for 1.5 days but all the craziness aside, Charleston was beautiful. It was so much cheaper than DC and their food was simply… comforting. Meaning loads of deep-fried dishes and delicious sweet tea that was basically pure sugar. Exactly what we needed after this crazy adventure.

We went to a brewery that night and I made Lola take obnoxiously cute pictures of me and Andrew. She was a good sport. Almost didn't complain about third-wheeling at all. She actually loved ganging up with Andrew and making fun of me. Sometimes I felt like I dated a male version of Lola. Just less egocentric.

In the morning we went to a local market and just wandered around. Some boys stopped us and tried to sell us a weird handmade flower. I automatically said "no thank you" but Andrew took me by surprise. He told them to wait for him, ran to the ATM and took out $50 to pay for the flower. No one had ever done something like that for me. If I wasn't already falling in love with him, I would have started to in that moment.

But the most fun part of that trip was our drive back home. We had some deeply inappropriate conversations. We talked a lot and we definitely found out some things about each other we never thought we would. Lola, as an addition to our trip, was slightly weird but extremely fun. She definitely had more courage to talk about sex and ask questions that would never have left my mouth. To my surprise, Andrew didn't mind answering them. It was also the time when everyone discovered that I was too shy to say "dick" and they kept teasing me until I said it a few times with a bit more confidence; I'm still ashamed of using such a vulgar word.

We spent 10 hours in the car together, which was a true bonding experience between the three of us. I was really impressed with how well Andrew handled Lola. About two hours from home, we drove straight into a snowstorm. I hadn't planned on staying overnight at Andrew's but that whole sex talk made me so turned on that I couldn't say no to him. I used the snow as an excuse for not coming back to my host family's house that night. And yes, having that one more night with Drew was totally worth it. Correction, we made sure to make it worth it.

The next day, I woke up super early and left him asleep in his bed just so I could get back to my host family's house in time for work. I got into the metro watching the outside world covered in snow. Every time I woke up next to Andrew, the world seemed to be just a bit better than it was the day before.

Love You, M

Have you ever been so in love that you just wanted to get on the top of a building and scream it out to the world? Well, welcome to the club! Falling in love usually makes you a bit pathetic and crazy. We all do crazy things for love, and one of them is annoying friends and family by constantly talking about the object of our affection.

Everyone knew that I loved Andrew before he did. It was my first serious relationship, so I had no idea when I should tell him. Definitely not the first time I felt it, which was less than a month into dating him. Probably not the second time, when I wasn't really sure what I felt. Maybe not even the third time when I knew - that was it. Looooove. Desperate for answers, I even googled it at some point.

So I dealt with these feelings as any other rational relationship first-timer would. I started telling everyone I knew but refused to be the one to say "I LOVE YOU" first. I also figured he loved me too because Lola said he admitted it on our way to Charleston while I was asleep. Clearly, I wasn't the only immature one in this relationship.

At some point my feelings got so strong that every time we had sex my mind was screaming "I LOVE YOU!" and I couldn't focus on anything else. I was petrified of blurting it out.

Then it kept hanging on the tip of my tongue. Andrew would say:

"Do you want some tea?"

My automatic reply would be "Sure, I LOVE YOU". Fortunately, I always stopped myself right before it came out of my mouth.

"I'm making dinner tonight," said Andrew.

"Oh, you're so sweet. I LOVE YOU!" - I wanted to scream.

My mind was so consumed by these words that they became a huge flashing sign in my head. Especially when I didn't want them in there. It felt like every time I talked to Andrew, the sign was popping up - making it impossible to ignore.

Finally, we got to March, and our weekend getaway in New York. I had probably never been as excited about going to New York as I was that day. I had very high expectations for that weekend. I wanted it to be perfect. And weirdly, it was.

We walked a lot. I was in so much pain because my boots were killing me. Still, for the first time in my life… I was falling in love with New York. Just the way I was in love with the boy walking right beside me.

It all started at the M&M store, which smelled like a freshly opened bag of M&Ms. Don't ask me why, but I absolutely loved it there and would visit with everyone every time I could - in New York or London. At some point, Andrew made a joke and I laughed. After all this time, I finally accidentally blurted it out:

"Gosh, I love you…"

There it was. I said it. I had tried so hard for all those months, and of course, I ended up being the first one to say it out loud.

"Fuck, I was joking!" I said quickly. You could see the confusion on his face. He didn't hear me. Or he did but he wasn't 100% sure that I actually said those words.

"What did you say?" he asked, smiling.

"Nothing…" I was so embarrassed.

He kept asking. All day long. We walked around Central Park and he wouldn't leave me alone. We got to a cute bridge with gondolas underneath and a small band playing romantic music on a violin and shit. That was it, I was sure he'd say he loved me too. But he didn't. He waited for ME to say it first. And I believed that I kind of already did, so I wasn't going to repeat myself. He knew exactly what I had said and at that point, he was just playing with me. We both were too stubborn for our own good.

I took him to my favorite spot, the Dumbo neighborhood. We ate some pizza and sat down by the river, overlooking the Brooklyn Bridge and the Manhattan skyline. We were so awkward. We both knew it was coming, and just like with our first kiss, we were both too freaked out to take that jump. Finally, after four months of being not so secretly in love with the Tinder guy… Andrew turned his face to me and said:

"Martyna, I love you."

Pause. Silence.

Still nothing.

My mind screamed "I LOVE YOU TOO!" but I was just staring into those beautiful brown eyes and realized that it was about to be my first "I love you" ever. I was freaking out. A lot.

He started babbling something, making it even more awkward, and I was just thinking "I LOVE YOU!!!" and "What the hell is wrong with me?! Just say it!".

Finally, when I thought I'd never speak again, I opened my mouth and choked out:

"You know I love you too, right?"

That was barely a declaration but hey, I did it! Kind of…

For the rest of the weekend, he kept on repeating it over and over. Meanwhile, I was still scared that if I said it to him, he wouldn't say it back. It didn't make sense but the fear was rooted so deeply within me, I couldn't just switch it off.

It took me a couple more months to actually say it without overthinking. I definitely wasn't a natural. Andrew also had to teach me how to hug. I was okay with quick "hi, how are you?" hugs but his hugs were long and intimate. Uncomfortable, if you asked me. It took me another few months to get used to those. Learning how to be in a relationship took me a really long time. To be honest, I'm not sure if I ever actually learned how to be good at that. As Lola pointed out, I was most certainly emotionally disabled.

#martinatravels

In November 2018, I did an online course as one of the au pair requirements. In order to pass it, I had to do some kind of volunteering.

So I signed up for volunteermatch.com and was surprised at how quickly I found a perfect opportunity for myself. It was a tour guiding position for a local hostel. Even better, I recognized its name. I had stayed with that organization many times while traveling (including the infamous bunk bed sex in Vancouver). I actually lived in one of their hostels for two weeks in London while waiting for my flat (apartment). Needless to say, they were a huge part of my life already, so this truly was perfect.

After a quick interview, I started volunteering as a tour guide. As predicted, I instantly fell in love with it. I loved interacting with people and sharing my new hometown with them. It was kind of crazy to think that I, a small-town Polish girl, was a local tour guide in the capital city of the United States.

This job was created for me! Well, “job” was a bit of a stretch. I wasn’t getting paid for it… unless you count the life experience!

Tour guiding became a huge part of my life, as I started doing it weekly. It also became an inspiration for MartinaTravels. In the beginning, it was just a hashtag I used for some of my travel photos. Then it evolved into a website that I created to share my tips for sightseeing in DC. Then I started posting more about my travels and how I organized my trips.

My dream was to open a big international travel company. I wanted to start it in a cafe - a place where people could visit and experience the world without leaving their town.

I remember the very first time I mentioned the MartinaTravels idea to Lola. I was so excited and she just said:

"Martyna, why do you think Steve Jobs didn't name all of his inventions "Steve Jobs"??? Do you think you could come up with something a little bit less egocentric?"

I looked at her and shook my head.

"It's gonna be MartinaTravels, whether you like it or not," I said, and for the first time in my life, I was so sure of what was going to happen. It was my destiny and I could clearly see my future.

In the end, Lola got used to my idea. Just as I expected, she did everything in her power to support me. We sat in my basement and worked on MartinaTravels together. She helped me with creating my website and the logo - I had no experience in running a website so she taught me a lot. She was amazing. She loved giving me a hard time but at the same time, she never hesitated to help me.

While I was waiting for my green card, I hoped to at least legalize MartinaTravels and make it a real company. But of course, without a work permit, I couldn't do that either.

So I decided to do it voluntarily. I offered free travel guiding services. And I did get a few "clients" before COVID hit and the whole travel industry fell apart. Some of them were from my previous tours for the hostel and some of them were just people who stumbled upon my website. Helping them out was exciting and rewarding for me even if I didn't get paid for it. I tried to treat every person like they were my real clients and MartinaTravels was a real company. I had business cards and stickers. I took them everywhere with me and spread them all over the US. I was a proud owner. I even got a MartinaTravels tattoo on my hip, underneath an airplane that was already there. Oh, to be 23 and so self-absorbed to name a company after yourself and tattoo it on your own body…

Host Family Issues

At the beginning, my host mom was very excited that I had started dating. They wanted to meet Andrew so badly and they were incredibly happy for me. They encouraged me to take a night off to go on a date. They didn't seem to have any issues with me coming back late either. I was never late for work and tried to respect them as much as possible. It seemed like the new dynamic of me dating didn't interfere with our relationship at all. So what went wrong?

For some reason, my host mom got it in her head that I didn't care about being an au pair anymore. She convinced herself that I just wanted to get out of there. At that time, that couldn't have been further from the truth. I spent most of my weekends at home, just not Saturday nights. I tried to be available as much as I could. But I wasn't there all the time that they seemed to want me to be. And that became the first issue.

Per program regulations, au pairs were supposed to work no more than 45 hours a week. Unfortunately, many of them had to work way more than that because their host families didn't care about the rules. I was lucky. Most days my host family simply didn't need me to work that much. Maybe I worked a bit more in the summer time or during the winter break. Besides that, I worked maybe about 25-30 hours per week. Which was not that much.

What au pairs were supposed to be, and what the whole program was based on, was being flexible.

But flexible is such a funny word. For me it meant willing to occasionally work overtime. Maybe start earlier or finish later. Meanwhile, for a lot of host families, it meant being available at any time of the day, very often with no heads-up. If we weren't willing to change all of our plans just to accommodate our host families' wants and needs, we were bad au pairs. At least that was the unspoken assumption of this program.

When I was 18, it honestly didn't bother me. I allowed my host family to constantly change my plans and was okay with having no idea of what my schedule would look like. I even worked on my 19th birthday - which was a Saturday, usually my day off - and pretended that I didn't mind. I spent half a day working and rescheduling my friend for hours while my host mom was shopping. And that was totally on me. I didn't say anything.

But then they invited me and my friend for dinner at my favorite Mexican restaurant. They bought me a cake with "Happy Birthday, Martyna!" on it and got me some really nice gifts. My host mom asked me for months what I wanted to get for my birthday or Christmas. They always made sure I felt like a part of the family. It was a really nice feeling.

The second time around, for my 22nd birthday, they gave me the whole weekend off and brought me cupcakes from my favorite bakery. Everyone knew it was my birthday, my host mom would be talking about it for a whole week. The kids signed cards for me. Mary helped me bake a cake for a road trip with my friends.

But then… the same host family completely skipped my 23rd birthday. I didn't get to blow out any candles, no cupcakes this time, no gifts either. The kids didn't even know that it was my birthday. It wasn't their fault. The parents were supposed to be the ones who told them but still, it hurt a lot. They gave me a day off and didn't bother to do anything nice the night before when I was working late for them. When I got back to work on Monday, I just found a card signed only by my host mom saying "Happy Birthday" and $50 attached to it.

The thing is I never wanted that $50. I never cared about the gifts. What I loved about them was that they made me feel like my birthday was as important as theirs. And I always returned the favor. I would buy some enormous balloons, bake or buy cakes, think about their gifts for months, and make sure the kids always had gifts for their parents. I'd even get a credit card from my host dad and make sure Kirsten was getting her perfect presents since he was too busy to get them on his own. I treated keeping Kirsten happy as part of my job.

It seemed like they were expecting the exact same person when I came back as a 21-year-old. I don't think they realized that, in the two years I was gone, I'd had a whole life and grown up a lot. They didn't like me having a boyfriend, but they also didn't like me having any plans at all. They wanted me to stay home all weekend the way I did when I was 18. Not for any particular reason, just as a backup in case they wanted to go out and didn't want to leave the kids alone. Clearly forgetting that the kids had grown up too, and they were definitely capable of staying alone for a couple of hours at home.

I started getting annoyed with their constant calls to check when I'd be home. I also didn't understand why they kept asking me to stay home when they clearly didn't need me. I did my best but I wasn't that shy 18-year-old who couldn't speak for herself anymore.

I guess my host mom had started to notice this, so she started getting annoyed with me. She started being mean about me having a boyfriend, throwing random jokes at me about getting married and having kids. She kept pointing out that I was already "checked out" and probably couldn't wait to leave. One time I mentioned that I wanted to stay in the US and go to college, instead of going back to Europe after the program. She looked at me and asked:

"Martyna, what are you doing with your life?"

It seemed like a fight I couldn't win. Considering the other circumstances - the drinking, the marriage drama - I gave up on them. Shortly after, I started seeing that my host dad stopped talking to me like he used to and pulled back as well. Mary wouldn't stop making mean jokes about Andrew. Josh started becoming a little Republican jerk who only talked about politics and didn't respect anyone besides his dad.

They were just kids, so I couldn't blame them. But I think I kind of did. I felt so unwelcome at the house I used to call home and it was breaking my heart. So I did the worst thing possible, I started pulling back from the kids. I even started to neglect the dogs. The dogs I loved and used to hang out with all the time. I barely walked Clem in the last few months of being an au pair. The worst part was that no one else besides me walked her either. They had got a new puppy a year earlier, and stopped taking care of Clem. The new puppy would pee everywhere, so they became so focused on walking her all the time that they forgot that Clem loved being outside as well. I felt so bad for distancing myself from everyone, but at that time, I was so unhappy. I couldn't help it.

But a lot of these issues were not just their fault, or mine. The core of the whole problem was the au pair program itself.

Their websites, Facebook pages, or even booklets, assured the parents that at any time they needed their au pairs, the girls would be there. And it was partially true. Yes, the au pair program was more flexible than any other forms of childcare. But we, au pairs, were not slaves. We had our own lives going on. We had friends, boyfriends, and hobbies. My host family wasn't just unhappy about me spending time with Andrew. Once, they actually forbade me from volunteering at the international exchange conference because they felt like it was "too time consuming". Another time, I had to cancel my tour for the hostel because my host dad had the WiFi guys coming over and apparently I was the only person "available" to let them in. When I told him I couldn't stay home because I was volunteering, he just got upset and replied:

"Martyna… What do you expect me to do now?!"

So I texted my mentor that I couldn't do the tour because I was sick. I couldn't tell her the truth. I was too embarrassed to admit my host family had so much power over my life. That I was canceling because of the stupid WiFi guys.

That kind of deal was unfair to everyone. It set unrealistic expectations, which allowed host families to think it was okay to expect the au pairs to be available at all times. And how could we ever say no to them? They hosted us in their homes, they gave us their food and paid most of our bills. The program made us completely codependent and a lot of host families used that advantage to get anything they wanted from their au pairs.

Losing Lola

As an au pair I had to get used to the fact that all the amazing girls I met throughout the program would leave at some point. All of us came to the US and went back home or somewhere else at different times of the year. None of my au pair friends decided to stay.

Losing Lola was honestly one of the hardest parts of my au pair year. I could deal with my host mom getting drunk and threatening to move out every week. I could deal with hours of boredom while taking care of the kids. But I had no idea how to move on from losing my best friend.

I cried for weeks after Lola went back to Spain. I didn't only lose my friend, I lost my favorite partner in crime. I was left alone and realized I basically only had my boyfriend left. Well, not exactly, but of course, there was no one like Lola.

Lola's departure made me closer to Andrew, though. We hung out more, planned trips together - basically became inseparable. Although, nothing could make up for the fact my best friend had moved across the ocean and I was forced to learn how to live without her.

In all honesty, I was kind of horrible at it. In the first months or maybe even year, I probably talked to her on the phone more than to Andrew, or any other person. We shared all of our thoughts with each other. We recorded 5-minute-long voice messages that were us just babbling the most random thoughts that made no sense. We probably talked just as much as when she was here. Maybe even more.

But it wasn't the same. I missed hanging out with my best friend. I wished things were different. I was convinced I couldn't survive without Lola in my life - or more specifically, without her being within driving distance.

When Lola left, I was so lonely in the whole "my host mom was an alcoholic" issue. Before, Lola was always there for me. Supporting me and helping me to get through the dark thoughts. But she was gone and no matter how much I loved talking with her on the phone, I needed someone who could be there for me, hug me, say it would be okay. So it was time to be honest, and share the truth with Andrew.

Telling him about Kirsten was not easy. Not at all. But it helped. I felt like it made our relationship stronger and finally, I had some kind of control over my life again.

Still, Lola was kind of the only reason why I had stayed with my host family in the first place. If not for her, I would have left the second I realized what I was dealing with. After she left, I realized I didn't want to be an au pair anymore.

One morning I was woken up by loud screaming. I had no idea what was going on. Very confused, I tried to listen to the yelling upstairs.

"It's your fault!!! You told your dad on me!"

I sat on my bed shaking and trying to figure out if I was supposed to call the police (my host dad was out of town), take care of the kids, or just wait until it passes. Mary came over to me crying and she said that Josh told his dad he heard Kirsten talking to a man on the phone.

After 20 more minutes of screaming, my host mum got dressed, came to the living room, and said:

"I'm sorry, I'm having a bad morning."

I didn't say anything. I was done. I looked at her and realized I hated her. For what she had done to the kids. What she had done to me. When they left for school and work, I tried to call Lola but I guess she was busy. I was so frustrated… I couldn't do it anymore. So I called my LCC and told her about everything...

What Happens in Vegas...

After our first "I love you's", the pressure of me leaving was hanging over our heads. I decided that going to college in the US was something everyone would benefit from. You know, I'd get a degree, and Andrew wouldn't have to leave everyone he loved just to follow me to Thailand. Plus, we both wanted to be done overthinking how to solve this problem and just enjoy each other's company.

So I focused on getting into Northern Virginia Community College. I got my English certification, and made my mom send me the transcripts of my high school diploma. I was so ready and beyond excited!

Meanwhile, I was planning a West Coast road trip with my big brother. We were supposed to meet up in San Francisco, rent a car, and travel around the West Coast's cities and the best national parks. That was my other obsession: planning road trips. I spent hours planning this trip and it ended up being a somewhat masterpiece of road trips.

However, something unexpected happened… I had a very hard time leaving DC. Specifically, Drew. We spent all night together trying to say goodbye, trying to make ourselves feel better, and basically stop being so pathetic. Being apart for three weeks shouldn't have been such an issue. But it was. Somehow, he had sneaked into my heart, put down his roots, and didn't want to leave.

It was really annoying. I mean, cute… we were in love and all that. But at the same time I had become that girl who can't even go for a trip without her boyfriend. I felt so lame but I couldn't help it. All I wanted was unlimited time with Drew. I was heartbroken to leave him behind and that feeling was overwhelming.

I started on my own in Portland and stayed there for a few days. I tried really hard to enjoy it as much as I could. I stopped myself from texting him too much and tried to be patient. After all, he was coming to Los Angeles to meet up with me and my brother and then we were supposed to drive to Vegas together. It was exciting! Yet, I couldn't get rid of that feeling that solo traveling would never be as fun as it used to be. I missed him so freaking much. I couldn't believe how lame I had become.

I kind of liked Portland. Emphasis on kind of. It wasn't easy, as a lot of times I was scared for my life. There were a lot of homeless people walking in the middle of the street and screaming. It wasn't a city where I'd feel safe after dark.

But then I did a free walking tour organized by my hostel and I realized that Portland had its charm hidden in the details. I walked past so many places by myself, barely noticing them or just thinking they were weird or cool. Then our tour guide took us to the exact same spots, and gave us stories behind them. Loads of stories about ghosts, witchcraft, clowns, or (weirdly) The Simpsons. According to our guide, out of all US cities, Portland had the most stripclubs per capita. There was also the World Naked Bike Ride that originated there. Personally, I was there for the donuts! Not the overrated and overpriced Voodoo Doughnuts. After trying many different ones, my favorite shop turned out to be the NOLA Doughnuts.

Finally, the time came and I left Portland. I got to San Francisco, ordered a beer and a glass of wine at the airport bar, and waited for my brother to find me. He landed only a few minutes after I did, so it didn't take him too long.

Not long after I got our drinks, I saw him squeezing through the crowd. He looked exactly the same as usual. Big guy with a ginger beard. He looked kinda lost, so I waved at him. We hugged, said "hi", and sat down with our drinks. We caught up before heading to our hostel.

My brother's name was Michal and he was as you could expect any big brother to be. Annoying, and gross. He drank way too much beer, ate way too many burgers and used to beat me up when I was a kid. He used to be a huge jerk to me but once I left for the States at the age of 18, he became nicer to me. I guess because he just started missing me. Since then, I always tried to invite him over to wherever I lived every year. I felt like without me he would never travel anywhere at all. Together we went to Dublin, Liverpool, London, Turkey, Greece, DC, NYC, and now to the West Coast.

We spent three nights in San Fran, but honestly the only thing I could focus on was the fact that Andrew was the next highlight on our itinerary. I was counting down the days and the hours. I basically accepted the fact I was full-on pathetic and decided to ignore the feeling of shame. I was in love… there were worse things than that.

If not for the enormous amount of homeless people and clear drug abuse, San Francisco would've been my dream city to live in. I had visited it a few times before and was never disappointed. Every single time, I discovered something new and interesting. I couldn't wait to take Andrew there one day and show him my favorite spots. I also never missed an opportunity to go to the Cheesecake Factory on top of the Macy's building. I couldn't care less about how overrated it was.

After San Francisco we were off to the City of Angels - Los Angeles. We arrived around 9 PM and were supposed to pick up Andrew from the airport right after midnight. I was so anxious that it started becoming a bit disturbing. It had only been a few days since I saw him. I shouldn't have been that excited - it was getting ridiculous. I took a shower, shaved my legs, and put my favorite dress on. I was ready!

We drove to the airport and Michal stayed in the car while I went to get Andrew. As soon as I noticed him waiting for his luggage, I couldn't help it - I jumped on him and hugged him like never before. It was insane, only a few days had passed and I missed him like it had been a year or something.

The first day and night were perfect. We stayed at Hosteling International in Santa Monica. We spent all day at the Universal Studios and went out to an Irish Pub with my brother in the evening. Right after my brother released us from our babysitting duties, we headed to the beach for a midnight walk.

All that being apart made our conversations really deep that night. We both didn't expect to feel the way we did. I definitely didn't. I guess that short time apart made us realize we were getting more serious than we thought we were. Per usual, we tried to keep it light, though. We still hadn't figured out how to make big relationship steps without the awkward silence and waiting for the other one to make their move. But that night on the beach… It wasn't awkward at all. It was just the two of us in the dark, with the waves crashing in the background.

We woke up the next morning, went back to the beach, swam in the ocean, and met up with my brother for breakfast.

Afterward, we headed to the Griffith Observatory where the famous Hollywood sign hike started. No one in their right minds would think of hiking for hours in 90 degrees in the full sun. The park ranger kept on driving past us, asking if we had enough water and were doing alright. He mentioned he had already had to rescue someone that day. The pictures from that hike were possibly the least attractive photos of me ever taken. Red face, and terror in my eyes caused by the thought of the second degree burns I was getting. I had a huge phobia of getting sunburnt. Surprisingly, I got none from that hike.

I made Andrew bring his guitar all the way to the top; and recorded a YouTube video of him teaching how to play "Fast Car" by Tracy Chapman with the Hollywood Sign in the background. I thought it was pretty cool. He thought I was crazy. But the views were just amazing, so I'd say I was right. The heat was killing us but we still made it to the top of the hill, behind the sign. The whole area was completely restricted and we couldn't get any closer to it. We enjoyed the views though and took even more unattractive photos of us, drinking the last sips of our water.

After the hike, completely defeated, we got back to the car and headed to Vegas. Well, only two of us were defeated. Drew was perfectly fine. With his dark skin and all that athleticism, he had no issues with the hike. Sometimes, it was really difficult not to hate him.

It took us a few hours to get to Vegas and traffic added an extra hour to our journey. Plus another hour for a "quick" stop at In'n'Out to get some calories in. Somehow we managed to almost run out of gas, so we found the most expensive gas station I had ever been to in my entire life. I guess they could set their own prices, since they were located in the middle of the desert and the only gas station nearby. It was a long day. By the time we got to our hotel, we were exhausted and definitely not up for partying all night. But for Andrew, it was the only night in Vegas, so we didn't really have a choice. He was heading back to DC the next day.

So we sucked it up, took showers, put semi-fancy clothes on, and hit the bars. I got one of the biggest margaritas they had, which was a huge bottle with a straw that screamed 'Vegas'. That was enough to get me through the night, keeping me tipsy at all times.

While the guys lost all of their money designated for Vegas, I won about $200 playing slots. Both of them were terrible gamblers and didn't know when to stop. It reminded me of the time Lola and I gambled in Atlantic City and I had to babysit her casino chips because she was ready to lose them all. Surprisingly, I was a semi-lucky gambler and usually (not always) knew when to stop.

Finally, we decided it was time to leave my brother behind - only after he promised he wouldn't spend any more money, and that he'd finish his drink and go back to his room.

We walked around the hotel, then went outside to the strip.

Once again, we started getting deep. I was so extremely sad that Andrew was leaving the next day. I tried not to cry all the time and it all felt so stupid. I couldn't help it, though. He was taking my heart back to DC and leaving my body completely alone on the West Coast.

We were standing on the hotel patio when, out of the blue, Andrew suggested:

"We should get this visa thing over with and just get married."

I looked at him and tried very hard not to say "Yes! Let's do it!". Instead, I asked:

"Is that your proposal?"

"No…" he replied, and we went quiet again.

We both were a bit drunk and super emotional about his departure. We definitely shouldn't be getting married. There was also a different part of my brain that was dancing around in a victory dance saying "He loves you, he wants to be with you, just do it!".

And I honestly would have, if he had proposed at that moment. If he had gotten down on one knee and asked me to marry him, I'd have said "yes" without any hesitation. I even secretly looked up the infamous Vegas wedding chapels to see if anything was open. But it was super late... or early, since we had just hit 4 AM and everything was either closed or too far away. And he didn't really mention it again. I knew if I ever married Andrew, it would be amazing and full of love and definitely not connected to any of my visa issues. That meant a real proposal that came from his heart. That's what I was waiting for. So instead of getting married, we just walked around - all sad and pathetic.

After another hour or two we got back to our hotel room. I wanted to have the best night ever so badly but I just kept crying because he was leaving in the evening. Finally, we fell asleep just so we could wake up two hours later, because there was no way I was letting Andrew come all the way to Vegas without seeing the Grand Canyon. And I had no shame in making my brother drive us while I slept on Andrew's lap in the backseat. A few hours later, we got to my least favorite part of the Grand Canyon, but unfortunately that's all we had time for.

To no one's surprise, I was super tired and unhappy all day long. I wanted to enjoy my last day with Drew, but I just couldn't. I kept thinking that it was his last day with me. And yes, I was fully aware that I was coming back to DC in about 10 days. I knew how pathetic it was, yet I also couldn't stop feeling like it was the worst thing that had ever happened to me.

All that time I was thinking that we should've gotten married. We should've just done it and then we'd be happy and ready to start our lives together. But we didn't. So I just kept walking around the Grand Canyon trying to smile and not randomly start crying in front of all those tourists. Also, I was super hot. Who the hell wanted to go to the Grand Canyon in August?! Oh yes, that was my idea. I was waiting in the line to get overpriced Gatorade. Finally I got so annoyed with waiting that I just sort of stole it from the fridge and walked away. For some reason, it made me feel better. For the first time that day I laughed. It felt good. Wrong type of good but better than the ball of miserability that I was before I became a Grand Canyon thief.

We drove back to Vegas and as usual, I let the guys drive while I slept in the back seat. Once we got back, we only had a few hours left until Andrew's flight. We were both so sad and pathetic… My poor brother probably had no idea what to do with this new version of his sister.

We were staying at the New York, New York hotel. Besides the casinos, there was also a mini roller coaster, mini Statue of Liberty, and of course - mini Brooklyn Bridge! As if we couldn't have been even cheesier, we went over there and just stood in silence for a moment. I wanted to come up with something smart to say. Something that wasn't:

"Hey! We've got 2 hours left! We can still get married!" or…

"I'll do anything, just don't get on that plane."

But instead, I said:

"You're the love of my life."

For the girl who couldn't even reply to his very first "I love you", that was a milestone. It seemed like we had traveled a million light years since that first time at the Brooklyn Bridge when I could barely admit I loved him. Andrew was shocked too, I could see he was. It had only been three months since New York but it felt like years had passed. That was me saying "Hey, maybe we didn't get married but you're the only one I could ever want anyway". He didn't expect that. But at least he knew how I felt.

We took an Uber to the airport and I didn't cry at all. Well, at least not in front of him. I burst into tears as soon as he walked away. I didn't think he'd see it but after crying for a couple of minutes in front of the building, I felt somebody's hand on my shoulder. Andrew was back. His face told me he felt the same way. Completely heartbroken and not ready to leave. We kept hugging and kissing and I promised him I'd be okay but I clearly wasn't. Then he left. Me on the other hand… I had no interest in continuing that trip. And that was coming from a person who made her whole life about traveling. I felt helpless.

I got back to the casino at our hotel and tried not to fall apart. I won another $300 and then lost probably half of it or even more. I didn't really count it at all. I was too depressed.

The next day, while my brother and I were having breakfast, I came up with a great idea. Well, a great idea from my perspective. In Lola's opinion, I was being a jerk for wanting to leave my brother alone just so I could come back a few days earlier to the love of my life. Well, she didn't put it in these exact words, but only because she didn't understand how desperately in love I was. Being away from Andrew hurt. I didn't want to hurt anymore. I wanted to be with him. I needed to be with him.

After talking to Michal, I booked tickets to DC. Our original plan was to travel around Arizona and Utah, then drive to San Diego, and back to San Francisco. I decided to skip the SD and SF parts. I asked my brother to drop me off at the airport in Vegas on his way to San Diego, and to continue our trip without me. I knew I was being unreasonable but I didn't care. All I cared about was Andrew.

For the next few days, instead of being all sad and moping around - I was excited about my surprise. Of course, I told everyone about it besides Andrew.

I understood why Lola was so mad at me for leaving my brother all alone in a country he didn't know and cutting our trip short. However, at least it let me focus on traveling with him and I didn't drive him crazy with my depressing mood. I was happy to be there as long as I could come home early and surprise Drew.

Overall, it was one unforgettable trip. We slept in a yurt in the middle of the desert; I was sure we were going to get killed either by a desert serial killer or one of the thousands of bugs in our little yurt. We kayaked through Lake Powell, hiked Bryce Canyon, explored Moab in Utah… It was hard to believe how far we had come from being two small-town Polish kids. I was so grateful - and ready to get back to the biggest blessing of my life at that time.

On the day of my departure, we made sure to have our last In'n'Out and I made sure that Michal knew where to go and what to do. He was actually pretty excited. He decided to go to Mexico one afternoon and enjoyed his time without me. I wouldn't have been able to go because of the visa restrictions for second year Au Pairs, so the whole situation turned out to be not that bad after all. He kept sending me pictures from touristy Mexican restaurants on the border.

I texted Andrew that it was my turn to drive so I wasn't going to respond for a while. He should've known better - it was never my turn to drive. Meanwhile, I got on the plane. I flew all the way to DC and got picked up by Steven's girlfriend. She was planning to spend the night at their house anyway, so it was a perfect solution.

We were pulling into the parking spot when I saw Andrew walking back from the gym in his shorts and a hoodie. I panicked and hid under the seat but then changed my mind and jumped out of the car. He had already passed the car, so I ran up to him from the back and crushed him into his body. He looked startled, probably thinking he was getting robbed, because the first thing

I saw was his angry and confused face. Then he realized that it was me and the anger was replaced with complete astonishment.

"What the hell?! What are you doing here?"

I pulled out a sign written on an old piece of a Corona 6-pack box saying:

"I choose YOU over San Diego. Every day, any day, forever and always."

For the next couple of days he kept looking at me and saying:

"I can't believe you're here. I feel like in a movie."

We also kept casually talking about the whole marriage thing. I knew we both wished we had more courage back in Vegas to admit that was what we really wanted. But just like in Vegas, we were too scared of what the other would think if we actually proposed marriage. So we just kept laughing it off and saying: "That would be crazy!".

I didn't tell my host family I was back early. All I wanted was some uninterrupted time with Andrew.

One night, we were watching a movie. It was just a couple of days after my surprise and Drew still couldn't believe I was there with him. He said no one had ever done anything like that for him. Unknowingly, I had made him fall for me even more. That was probably the reason why, out of nowhere, Andrew stated:

"Fuck it, I'm doing it!"

He stood up and got me up as well. Then he got down on one knee. He was saying how much he loved me and how much he wanted to be with me but honestly, I blacked out. I could barely hear him through the crazy thoughts running through my head. Finally, he asked:

"Martyna Nowacka, will you marry me?"

I could barely speak through the heart palpitations but I did start nodding and I was pretty sure I said "YES".

I was wearing a navy dress with watermelons on it. I had got it about a month before - after we ran through a storm and got completely soaked. The next day I had no clothes to wear so I bought that dress from the GAP near his place. That would always be my engagement dress.

The craziest part was that throughout all of it, Steven had been upstairs with his girlfriend. I was so excited and started getting a bit loud, so Andrew shushed me - pointing upstairs. It was our night, Steven didn't have to be a part of it. At least not yet.

Either way, we were engaged. It was completely crazy but real. Not even a year into a relationship and we already knew that we wanted to spend the rest of our lives together. Yes, we were young and naive. I knew it wasn't going to be easy. That sometimes it would be damn tough. But I also knew something else. That crazy spontaneous proposal in their living room would always be one of the best moments of our lives.

Last Month

That last month as an au pair with my host family was not easy. When I told them I was moving out, it felt like they were shocked. Like it was the very first time I'd ever told them about it.

But it wasn't. I'd been telling them about us looking for an apartment for months. I was pretty sure the very first time I mentioned the move was back in the summer! And suddenly we got to October and they were shocked.

I couldn't do much about it. After telling my LCC about all the issues, my host family pulled away. They convinced me to stay with them and finish my au pair year but I could see they didn't want me there anymore and I had no power left to deal with it.

So we found an apartment about 40 minutes away from DC and were about to move in soon. But since my living situation seemed to be getting worse day by day, Andrew told me I could move in with him and Steven for a couple of weeks before heading to our new apartment. And I liked that idea.

I wanted to move on with my life so badly but I felt like I couldn't as long as I lived with my host family.

I was planning to keep working for them for another couple of months and we seemed to have an agreement that I'd be able to use the car and work only in the afternoons. Well, I thought we did.

As I said, when they realized it was time for me to move out, they were not happy with me at all. My host mom started changing her mind every five minutes about my car privileges and about when they would need me to work.

I ended up waking up every day at 5:50 AM to get there by 6:45. They knew perfectly well it took me around 30 minutes to get to their house from Andrew's but they couldn't care less. Maybe it all would make sense if I was actually working in the mornings. But my only responsibility was to get the kids to school. Most of the time my host parents had plenty of time to do it by themselves. They made me go there simply to prove a point. Also, I couldn't use the car anymore because apparently theirs was not meant to do such long distances every day so I had to start borrowing Andrew's car. Finally I just got my own, which made me forever poor, but that's a different story.

I survived a month of that craziness before I broke, and told them a complete lie just to get out of that situation. I felt terrible about lying and I knew they would never forgive me. For over a year they had been my priority but it had to come to an end. For once, I had to put myself first.

*****

I woke up in the morning and realized what day it was. It was that day. I had been waiting for it for a very long time. I couldn't believe it was finally here. It seemed crazy... but yes, it was my last day as an au pair.

I never expected things to go the way they did. The first time I left my host family was heartbreaking, but I knew they would always be in my heart and I'd be in theirs. I knew we'd have many opportunities to meet each other again. This time I was simply exhausted, unhappy, and ready to never see them again.

But once I picked the kids up from school, I tried to feel a bit better about everything. I wanted them to have good memories of me. The last few months were difficult, and I let my personal feelings get to me and stopped being there for them as much as I should've been. I've got to be honest, I felt like an unwanted stranger in a place that I used to call home and it hurt like hell.

But I decided to get over it and move on. Make that last day count.

We got home and I started cooking up some dinner. I was in the middle of stirring pasta when my host mom texted me that she'd be home soon with my last check and ready to pick up the family phone from me.

Let me point out, I'd been using that phone for almost two years and my whole life was in there. But that wasn't a problem. The problem was that the very next day, I was supposed to pick up my parents from the airport in New York and I didn't have a chance to get a new phone, since my parents were bringing me one from Poland. I just assumed that my host family wouldn't mind me keeping it for a few more days since they knew me and had treated me like family since I was 18. But I was wrong. Very firmly, my host mom texted me back saying that there was no way I could keep the phone even for a day longer since they needed it for the new nanny.

Okay, so I didn't know the real story behind it, but I was 99% sure they hired an American girl or someone like that who already lived in the USA and had their own phone. They didn't need it right away. However, they wanted to prove a point and they did.

When Kirsten got home, she didn't even bother to pretend she cared about me leaving. It was all business for her. Getting rid of another employee.

Right away she took the phone away from me and asked for (or more like requested) my new address. I looked at her suspiciously and asked why she needed it. She replied:

"Just in case you don't quit the gym in time, I want to send you a bill for the next month."

Wait, what…?

These people started hosting me at their house for the first time when I was 18. They were acting like my parents. Then when I left, we were constantly emailing and they even visited me in London right before I came back to the States.

They were so excited for me to move back to their house. They also paid for all my bills and gym membership like a lot of host families did. Sometimes they would joke about adopting me because, apparently, I was so amazing!

However, now I was not even trustworthy enough to cancel the gym membership that they put on their credit card.

For me, the whole situation was just ridiculous. Honestly, I lost any trust in their good faith. I took a piece of paper and wrote some random non-existent address. I wanted to make sure they wouldn't be able to track me down.

Too much? A bit paranoid? Probably. Yet… how satisfying. At that moment, I simply knew I never wanted to see them again. It was sad, I really loved them at some point in my life but the whole second time at their house as an au pair was terrible for me. I tried so many times to fix it or leave before things got really bad but they didn't want me to go. They ignored every single issue they had and were ready to live and enjoy that illusion they thought their life was. I just couldn't support it anymore.

I said my goodbyes to Kirsten and the kids. My host dad was not at home, which was not surprising at all. No one seemed really touched by the fact it was my last day with them. Three years ago, I got a cake, a last dinner with the kids in our favorite restaurant, and loads of hugs. Now I just got "See you around" and "Bye".

Once I got into my car I quickly realized there was a rainstorm and, if I got lost or took a wrong exit without a phone, I'd be totally lost. I hated driving in the rain already (or just generally) and this was not helping. I started freaking out since I couldn't let anyone know that I was on my way home, and I couldn't use GPS to get to the apartment that we had just moved into a week before. There was huge traffic, and people were going crazy because no one could see where they were going. I wanted to cry so badly.

I was exhausted and stressed out like never before, but couldn't get any tears out which was weird because usually, I'd cry in the car all the time.

Finally, after an hour and a half (it would be 40 minutes without traffic but commuting in northern VA sucks…) I got home. Andrew wasn't there. I sat down on my laptop and tried to log into my Instagram to let him know I was home. Of course, only then I found out that messaging on IG was only possible from their smartphone app.

I knew it was highly possible he wouldn't open his inbox in time but I wrote him an email saying I was all safe and waiting for him at home. I stayed on the couch and just stared at the wall.

About 10 minutes later I heard the door opening and Andrew walked into our living room with a look of pure fright on his face. I ran into his arms and started crying like a child.

"I was so worried," he said. "I tried to call but someone switched off the phone."

After a few minutes of crying, I explained to him the whole situation. I realized that my host family hadn't only let me drive straight into the storm without any way to reach other people, but also switched off the phone while my fiancé was trying to make sure I was alive.

We got ready and drove to the only Sprint location that was open to get me a new phone. At that moment, I just tried to ignore the fact that my parents were bringing me another one the next day and it was a huge waste of money. I knew there was no way I could drive to NYC without a phone.

By the time we got back home, it was after 11 PM, and I had to mentally prepare myself for driving all the way to JFK to get my parents the next day. Have I mentioned I hate driving?

Welcome to Paradise

By November 2019, both Andrew and I had quit our jobs. We decided to go for a three week pre-honeymoon to Hawaii - which was the best decision we could ever have made. It was possibly the best trip of our lives. Calling it a paradise wasn't an exaggeration at all, it really was a little piece of heaven on Earth. Also, it was the very first time we had spent so much time together and didn't get any break from each other at all! Living together could be hard, but in my opinion, traveling was much harder! Especially traveling on a budget.

While we were living together, we got to spend some time alone. We either hung out in different rooms or had different work schedules. But traveling was different. We usually shared a room, not an apartment. That meant no separate spaces to do our own thing. We didn't get to just go to the fridge and eat whatever we wanted. We had to coordinate and go to places we both liked.

We also very quickly realized that sharing a tent wasn't as romantic as we imagined. Nor was sharing a twin bed in a hostel. Plus when we fought, we were still stuck on the same trip. So the only thing we could do was walk twenty feet apart.

We've shared so many awkward and great moments at the same time. We fought a lot. Spent way too much money. Went on over 10 hiking trips. Had sex at least once every single day. Did sunset skinny-dipping on a private beach. And we "broke into" the Turtle Bay hotel. Well, we didn't actually break in. Just swam in the pool meant only for their guests.

Hawaii was incredibly diverse. Every island, every town, every hike was different. There were beautiful days that we never wanted to end and there were gloomy days that kind of made us freeze.

My favorite days in Hawaii were when we just took our rental cars and simply explored the islands. We drove between local towns - stopping wherever we wanted. I kept forcing Andrew to play guitar on random beaches so I could record more cool YouTube videos. Clearly, I had no idea we needed a proper microphone for those types of adventures. We ate from food trucks when we wanted to take a break from the overpriced groceries. We could rarely afford eating at restaurants, but we didn't mind. Eating cold spaghetti from tupperware on one of the most beautiful beaches we've ever been to was definitely a priceless memory.

On our last night in Maui, we went to a Luau - a traditional Hawaiian dinner. We got real fresh Lei - Hawaiian flower necklaces - and watched all the cool traditional dances. The food wasn't that great, but we got quite tipsy very quickly and finished the night off at the beach. We knew we couldn't bring the Lei back home with us, so instead we took it apart. With each flower we threw into the ocean, we said one thing we were grateful for. People were passing us by, probably thinking we were crazy. They were right. The next day we woke up exhausted, but still decided to get one last hike in before we headed to the airport.

In my opinion, traveling was just like living together. Only ten times more intense. We dealt with each other's grumpiness and hangriness, and we created the craziest memories - like mud fights in the most remote hiking spots we had been to. I had never expected to find a travel buddy for life but I felt so damn lucky that I did.

Cycle of Self-Pity

God, it was cold!

It had been a bit less than a week since Andrew and I had come back from Hawaii, and I had been freezing ever since. I was standing in front of the DMV, hoping to renew my driver's license. Unfortunately, they seemed to be oblivious to the idea of keeping their customers warm.

After standing in the outside line for 10 minutes, I went into the building and stood for about a few seconds in another line before a nice lady who worked there came up to me and asked what I needed from them.

I started explaining my situation to her. My visa was expiring on Christmas Day (the best time of the year, isn't it?), and because of that, my temporary driver's license was expiring as well. I needed to get a new one and even though I hadn't got a new status yet, I was here legally. I had applied for a green card and all that. She said, apologetically:

"I'm sorry but unless you show us a letter from the government confirming a status change or that you applied for a green card we can't renew your license."

I smiled and said it was okay. Because what else was I

supposed to do?

As I walked back to the car, I tried to convince myself that I was alright. I had known there was a possibility of me not getting a renewal. I was prepared for that. Yet, it didn't change the fact that it was another obstacle in my way that month.

I was jobless and had spent all of my savings on the car, apartment, and our pre-honeymoon in Hawaii. I was about to be short on rent and had no idea how to tell Andrew that I spent a bit too much on Christmas decorations and presents for him and his family. I sucked.

I had hoped that at least with a renewed license I would have been able to drive legally, but apparently, I wasn't able to do that either. Tears started going down my cheeks and there I was, crying again in that stupid nice but expensive car.

I switched the music off on my way home, and tried to figure out what I was gonna do. I lived in Northern Virginia, in a place where public transportation didn't exist. I needed to drive to places. It felt like it was going to be a constant stress from then on. I knew that every time I drove, I would be worried that I'd get pulled over without any form of valid identification

By the time I got home, I was already in a cycle of self-pity. I started thinking about being unemployed again and about how useless I was to Andrew in our relationship. I went on sittercity.com and tried to look for nanny jobs but as usual, I came to the same conclusion. First, it was illegal, and second, I hated the thought of taking care of children again. I had been an au pair for way too long and I couldn't imagine working with kids anymore. It was just not for me.

I pulled the leftover pizza out of the fridge and sat down on our super expensive leather couch to catch up on some shows and eat my breakfast. I felt pathetic and useless. I started looking up flights to London…

I did it from time to time. When everything sucked and I had no more strength, I opened my Expedia app and checked the flight prices. I wasn't proud of it but it kind of made me feel better. Like

I had a choice. That I wasn't a prisoner in my own world. I could escape whenever I wanted to. Wherever I wanted to.

But then, I started thinking about Drew. How amazing he was. How he made me smile and laugh. And felt embarrassed... about how much I loved him. I knew he was the one. He was my soulmate and there was no way in the world that there was any other guy out there for me.

Usually, that was the moment when I'd get up and start being productive. However, that day, it took me a whole episode of CW's 'Legacies', two slices of leftover pizza, and loads of Kinder chocolate to actually start doing something. Once I got up, I opened the curtains, switched on my laptop, and started paying the bills with the very little money I had left. Then I called my credit card provider and asked for a credit limit increase.

When Andrew came home, he went completely crazy on me. I guess I had freaked him out with my depressing messages, so he didn't stop hugging me. Then, he forced me to dance to Christmas music until I screamed in pain because I possibly broke something in my ankle while jumping. He carried me to the bed and didn't listen when I said I was okay. He brought frozen shrimp and placed it under my foot (not the aching one). Finally, he handed me a huge cup of tea and sat down on the couch and started our favorite show, 'Ink Master'.

And that's how I went from being productive (for five minutes) to napping on the couch with the love of my life.

Also, that's how all my meltdowns ended. No matter how depressed I was, or how defeated I felt, Andrew was always there to make me forget about everything and feel sane again. I couldn't imagine doing this whole process with anyone else but him.

Drew

When I think of Andrew Dearing, most of the time I don't think about how hot he is. And yes, he is super hot. Nah, I think about his goofy moves, stupid jokes, awkward questions, and puppy dog eyes.

There are only a few people in the world who can make me laugh when I'm mad and Drew is one of them. No matter how angry I am at him, he's always able to crack me up which, a lot of times, is even more annoying.

Andrew is the most obnoxious person I know and he's well aware of that. Also, feeding him takes up most of my money, and I'll never stop wondering how anyone can be so healthy and so not at the same time.

He's a personal trainer and an aspiring musician. He's a family person, and before I met him, I never would've thought that could be a sexy trait in a guy. Not at all. Yet here I am, and honestly, I love hanging out with his family.

Andrew always makes me feel like we're in a movie. He makes me imagine songs being played while we're walking and reminds me of amazing places I've been to while we're having sex.

He also breaks my heart every time we fight or with every unkind word.

Andrew is my travel buddy.

He's my inspiration.

My daily routine.

He's 90% of my grocery store run.

But he's also the one who'll carry the bags upstairs.

Drew is the noise I fall asleep to.

He's the only face I could ever wake up to.

He's my Chick-fil-A at 10 PM buddy.

He's my bad boy made in heaven.

He brings me a wet towel when I have a migraine.

He teaches me patience (work in progress).

And that hugs don't have to be uncomfortable.

He introduced me to 'Ink Master'.

And Japanese tattooing.

He makes me question everything I thought I had figured out.

Andrew Dearing is my soulmate and that's about it.

Illegal Shit

Right after we came back from Hawaii, I found a job. I was ready to give up on finding a job other than babysitting, but one day Andrew and I were picking up pizza and I saw the HELP WANTED sign. I went into the restaurant very quickly, got their contact details and the next thing we knew, I had started my training.

It was just a 10 minute walk from our place. It wasn't a great job, it paid very little and wasn't even close to what I wanted to be doing in life. But it paid the bills. At least part of them… a very small part. That's all that mattered.

That was how I became a "Pizza Girl".

Unfortunately, they did taxes for me so the government was officially informed that I was working illegally. Since there was a paper trail, there was no going back. So I decided to keep the job for a couple of months. At least until the wedding. I hated the fact that I had to do it. I hated doing illegal things. And mostly I hated that I felt bad for doing something that shouldn't feel bad at all.

I was really trying. Every day I tried to do good, and to be a good person. Yet, here I was doing illegal shit. And I couldn't believe that out of all the illegal things in life I could be doing, finding a job was one of them.

I had a choice when I married Andrew and we started our life together. I could either sit at home, do nothing, and, in the government's eyes, do everything the right way. OR I could find an illegal job and help Andrew with the bills. It wasn't really a choice. I knew I couldn't let him be the only one working for our brand new little family.

I looked into the consequences of working without a work permit and the Internet said it could be anything. From being deported and banned from the USA for up to 10 years, to just getting away with it as long as I didn't work for more than 180 days.

I kind of liked my new job. It was a small local pizza place, and it gave me the perfect amount of free time to focus on writing this book. They also gave me a free lunch every day which was absolutely delicious. Besides coming back home to Andrew, that was the most exciting part of my day. Also, him visiting me at work. Every time he came through that door, my heart was full. For the first time in a while, I found something I enjoyed doing. I liked dealing with the customers, meeting new people every day, and my new coworkers. They were young people in their high school or college years. For once, I was the grown up one. It was lighthearted and fun. Honestly, it would have been a perfect job if they'd paid me about three times more than they did.

My issue was that I felt like I was doing something really bad by working illegally. But the truth was - for many foreign communities in the US this was completely normal. They helped each other with finding jobs that paid cash so the illegal workers didn't have any issues with the government. It was a whole system of illegal workers who, somehow, were making way more than Andrew and I combined. Meanwhile, we were struggling because we were trying to do everything "the right way".

For me, it was very difficult to find any job. I didn't know anyone who could help me with finding a job that paid cash besides babysitting, and I really would've rather died than take care of kids again. I asked my lawyers once if I could at least start creating my own company. Not to earn money on it, but at least start setting it up. They said it was too risky and I should definitely wait for the work permit.

I just didn't get it. I wasn't an illegal immigrant. From the very beginning, since I came to America, I had done everything legally, and all according to the immigration laws. But at some point, the rules just didn't make sense anymore.

The rules wanted me to wait five to seven months for a work permit. They wanted me to be married, start a new life, and a new family, but also to stay unemployed for half a year. That was bullshit.

So there I was, working illegally just to be able to support Andrew with all of our expenses. Scared that any day someone could come in and ask for my work permit... arrest me, deport me. I was way over my head. I was just a Polish girl who fell in love with an American Tinder guy. How did I end up working illegally in a suburban pizza place?

Welcome to my American Dream...

The Au Pair Bubble

It was always easy to complain about being an au pair, especially when things at home were not going that well. But the truth was, being an au pair came with a lot of perks.

I had a big room all to myself, in a very nice Washington, DC house. No rent, no bills. A swimming pool in the backyard that was open all summer, which magically cleaned itself. A new phone with all the data and unlimited texts. A very nice car, that I could kind of call my own, was there for me at almost any time I needed it. Sometimes I just had to put some gas in it. Most of the food I ate came from my host family's fridge. It was a good life. A bubble, you could say.

Getting out of that bubble was not easy. To my surprise, I learned that people usually paid for their own phones. Or that to have a car, I had to buy a car. Also, apparently in the real world, a new laundry detergent didn't just magically appear on the shelf once I used all of it. I had to get it in my free time and pay for it with my own money. These were the very basic things that as an au pair I never worried about.

So I could easily complain for hours about being an au pair and getting only $250 a week. The truth was though, if the host family wasn't horrible, the au pair's life wasn't that bad either.

Unfortunately, breaking out of my bubble didn't only mean discovering the basic rules of adulthood. It also meant that I officially became an immigrant. I was legally permitted to stay in the USA, but that was about it. I didn't have a work permit or a student visa that would allow me to at least go to college. I wanted to apply for a student visa before Andrew proposed, but that wouldn't have made our situation easier. Probably even harder. Waiting to change my visa status - from au pair to a student - could take from five months to even a year. And I wouldn't have been able to work outside of the campus anyway. Getting married made so much more sense. We knew we wanted to spend the rest of our lives with each other anyway.

In order to leave my host family, I had to make sure I had a place to go, some way of transportation to get around, and money to support myself while waiting for a work permit.

Money was "easy". I got it from my parents (even if I felt a bit funny about it) and put it in a savings account. Well, I ran out of it pretty quickly but that's not important.

Getting the apartment was a nightmare, though. Andrew and I loved the idea of staying close to DC, preferably in Old Town Alexandria where he already lived with his roommate. What we realized quite quickly was that they paid the cheapest rent in Alexandria. If we wanted to live anywhere other than falling apart mice-invaded townhouses with occasional cockroaches as residents, we had to rethink our budget. Sadly, Alexandria was definitely above our budget - particularly as I wasn't going to be able to find a real job any time soon.

We started looking further and further down into Virginia.

But the limited budget wasn't the only issue for us. Getting a place in America was much harder than in Poland. Or maybe it wasn't, and in Poland I just had my mom's help. This time we had to prove we were able to pay for it. That meant bank statements, pay stubs, and a confirmation that we actually had jobs. And surprise, surprise! No one considered being an au pair a real job.

Since I didn't have any bills and didn't have rent to pay, my "pocket money" was ridiculously low compared to a minimum wage. Not even close to an average American income. I had no way to prove that I was able to pay the other half of our rent. I only had my savings account statements and no one wanted to accept them.

Finding a place that would accept our poor but lovely asses (forgive my language) took us over a month. We were stressed out, and I felt super frustrated with my life situation. In the end, we got an apartment that was affordable and accepted all of my crazy paperwork. It would have been perfect if not for the fact it was about an hour from DC. And I hated the town where it was located. But besides those little details, it was almost ideal.

Since we moved to a place that no one outside of Virginia had ever heard of, it was time to get a car. I loved the idea of owning a vehicle. It made me feel very grown up and like I achieved something in life. I didn't love the idea of paying for it though. It was a nice car and the monthly payment was kind of killing me. Actually, that's how you could describe my life at that time, especially the wedding planning. Or every piece of furniture I purchased. All of it was so nice, but I was definitely paying the price (rhyme not intended).

Getting a car was not easy either. Andrew had to cosign a loan for it because once again, no one thought being an au pair was a job. It took loads of paperwork and printing out all of my bank statements again, just to hear that I couldn't get it without my fiancé signing all the paperwork for me. I was exhausted from explaining my life and financial situation to strangers. I felt like I was set up for failure from the very beginning. Not just me, though. Andrew was affected by my situation too. It sucked.

The whole process of getting out of my "au pair bubble" made me realize I had no worth in the American system. As an immigrant without a work permit, I could only wait for months and do nothing. For such an independent person like myself, it almost felt like a life sentence.

That's exactly why every time Andrew went to work, I ended up in Starbucks next to his gym - writing a book that I expected no one besides my friends and family to read. I never thought I'd make money on it. I just had literally nothing better to do than to sit and write down my story.

I had reached a point where I had spent my last savings and I had no idea how I was going to pay for my credit cards the next month. I struggled to figure out how to pay our rent or if we were able to pay another wedding deposit that was coming up in two weeks.

After almost two years of being an au pair, I seemed to face new obstacles every day throughout the process of becoming a regular American resident. I wanted to overcome the dark thoughts. I wanted to be a better, more cheerful wife to Andrew, but I also felt useless and frustrated.

If you had asked me back then whether staying in America after being an au pair was worth it - I'd have said it was not. The only thing that made it all worth it to me was Andrew. And still, it didn't make it easier at all. I had never felt so helpless, so worthless, so trapped while I waited for the work permit.

It was a crazy thing to admit, but I didn't appreciate the au pair program enough. Living here and not being an au pair was freaking tough.

I just couldn't understand how the US government expected newly married couples to survive when one of them had no way to provide for the family. How could they expect someone to wait five to seven months just to simply work? When did work become a privilege? Wasn't it a human right? I didn't get it. It wasn't fair.

The car was great, and the apartment was great… I just had no idea how to enjoy this whole new life when it felt like I was in limbo… waiting for it to start.

Money, Money, Money

Back when I was in London, I heard about a class action lawsuit that a former au pair had started. I was very surprised about it - I knew a lot of au pairs were complaining about not being treated well and not earning enough money, but I didn't really get it.

I considered my au pair experience to be a really good one, so participating in that lawsuit felt wrong. I didn't feel like I had any reason to be "compensated" for my year in America. I loved my host family and even if they were not always fair to me or sometimes a bit annoying, I considered them a permanent part of my life.

Also, working in the United States for a year opened many doors for me in Europe. That's exactly why I couldn't imagine going against the program that had changed my life completely. I felt like opportunity after opportunity was waiting for me. I was all set. I didn't need that lawsuit or their money to make up for anything I went through. I just appreciated that I got a chance to be a part of this program.

However, things changed when I came to live with my host family for the second time. It was around February or March 2019. Every au pair's favorite time of the year: the tax return season. Don't be naive, there was no 'return' for the au pairs. Not only did we have to pay our taxes every year, but we also needed to fill out all those complicated forms by ourselves.

When I was an au pair for the first time, our community counselor helped us with that and explained everything. However, during my second time around, that was no longer an option. I guess for some legal reasons, but still.

Imagine all these international girls, who probably never had to fill out any tax forms before, left alone to do all of it on their own... Every March, every year. As a reminder, some of them were only learning English. We did have the option to hire a tax company to do it for us for about $100 but for us, even that was really expensive.

We belonged to the lowest tax bracket, obviously. We made a maximum of $12,000 a year, and instead of a salary, they called it our 'pocket money'. We then had to pay 10%, or roughly $1000, to the government.

They refused to call it a "paycheck", "salary", or "wage" because then the host families would be the ones paying taxes on our behalf. They would also have to pay us the minimum wage. So according to law we were not "working" nor were we getting "paid", but we still had to pay taxes like everyone else.

When I came to America for the first time, taxes were much lower. Then Donald Trump took over and they went up significantly. In 2016, I had to pay only $200 and that already seemed a lot to me. Many girls refused to pay taxes because they felt like it was too much for them or the process was just too complicated and exhausting, which was fair enough.

At the beginning of my au pair year in June 2018, my LCC was telling me all about it. Sitting next to me, Kirsten said:

"Don't worry, I will pay for the tax company to do the taxes for you."

Per usual, Kirsten loved pretending that she was such a kind person. Sometimes, it felt like she wanted to convince herself more than others. I really think she believed she'd help me when she said that. I smiled and thanked her.

March 2019 came very quickly. No matter how many times I hinted to Kirsten that I couldn't afford the tax return and that I was really struggling financially, she never remembered her promise. She just kept telling me how they were in a worse position than I was. I highly doubted that.

While I was struggling with taxes, I got Lola's text about the class action lawsuit. I thought about the fact that I was about to lose a month's worth of paycheck for something that didn't benefit me. That was also the first time I started doubting the greatness of this program. The possibility of getting money for the abuse that au pairs were experiencing didn't seem that crazy anymore.

I realized that I had spent almost a year with an alcoholic who, despite all the help I offered, recently started hating me for no reason (or just because I had a boyfriend). I was in an abusive situation and my host family was the one to blame. I realized the au pair program had failed me.

Was it my fault for not reaching out for help? Yes, definitely.

However, my host family should have never put me in that position in the first place.

I joined the lawsuit.

A few months later, I found out that we won and we were getting the money. I definitely needed it. At that time I already lived with Andrew and we were getting ready for a very expensive wedding. Plus another tax season was approaching...

I couldn't stop wondering, though… how many other girls were treated the way I was or even worse? How many of them were not lucky enough to have someone to pull them out of their misery?

If you asked me…that money didn't fix anything.

Did I appreciate having some extra money to pay for the wedding? Yes, definitely. Did it fix the fact that I had been put through hell by my host family, or the fact that they never even apologized or took accountability? Not really.

In the summer of 2019, I contacted my community counselor and told her all about the alcohol issue at our home. I was ready to leave that house but my host dad promised me to fix everything and convinced me to finish the program with them. The counselor kind of just let it happen. She knew how mistreated I was and let them stay in the program.

She knew and did nothing about it.

Honestly, there's no money in the world that could reimburse me for those nights when I went to bed, listening to the screams upstairs, wondering if my drunk host mom would get mad and hurt me or the kids while I was asleep.

Take Two on New Year's Eve

I had always hated New Year's Eve. Well, hate is a big word. Maybe I just didn't appreciate it as much as others did. To me, it was a day when most people had crazy hopes or expectations. Then they ended up unhappy with their night - standing in a long line for a crappy overcrowded club that nobody actually wanted to be in.

My first New Year's after Lola left was tough. I was upset all day because I was missing her. I knew it was probably very annoying to Andrew and because of that, he wasn't having a great day either.

I felt bad for ruining our New Year's Eve. At the same time, it was a day I usually would've spent partying with my friends, and back then, all of them lived across the ocean.

I could talk about how it sucked to be an au pair for an alcoholic. I could talk for hours about how difficult it was to live in the USA without a work permit and any possibility of finding a job. I could also tell everyone how complicated and stupid the green card process was.

But at the end of the day… I just missed my friends. And not many people in my life could understand it. Being an au pair was not easy. All the girls came to America at different times and all of us had to leave at some point. Out of everyone I met when I was an au pair, I only had one friend who was still in Virginia, Aroa. All the other au pairs had already left.

Andrew kept telling me that I should find more friends. Or that I already had friends - who were his friends' girlfriends. I wished it was as easy as in kindergarten when I could go up to a random kid and ask, "Can you be my best friend?". Unfortunately (for many reasons), we were not in kindergarten anymore and I didn't know how to make real friends. I knew some people in the US. But how was I supposed to turn those acquaintances into real friendships?

To be fair, Lola was also irreplaceable. Part of me was just being stubborn and holding people to an impossible standard of being my Lola 2.0. I wanted a friend who'd get on a plane and spend 24 hours in Nashville with me just because it was my birthday. I wanted someone to spend a whole New Year's Eve cooking and making a huge pot of Sangria with me. I needed a "let's go to Lincoln Memorial at sunrise for no reason" kind of friend.

Lola always made sure that every little thing was celebrated properly and I loved that about her. All those little quirky things for birthdays that people hate: huge balloons, surprise parties, unicorn cakes… I was that lame girl who wanted all of it and Lola got me.

And yes, we kind of had a toxic relationship. Our highs were high and our lows were very very low. We fought badly, and for reasons I can't remember we even slapped each other once or twice. Also, she always told everyone every inappropriate thing about me that she could remember. Especially when Andrew and I started dating. She had no filter and shared all my secrets with everyone. She hurt my feelings a lot. And yet, I couldn't live without her.

I kind of expected Andrew to step into Lola's shoes. I wanted him to throw me surprise parties, have the most fun New Year's Eve plans ever… I wanted him to buy me balloons for my birthday. When he didn't, I was disappointed and wished Lola was still here. Or that I could move back to Europe and be with her. That's exactly what happened that New Year's Eve. Andrew had nothing planned and he was the one with friends in this relationship. So we had a fight. I was grumpy and unhappy. He had no idea how to make me feel better because again, he wasn't Lola. I went to sleep early and that's how our 2019 ended.

On January 1st, we woke up in semi-crappy moods. This time, though, Andrew was committed to making the previous night up to me. He insisted we did a 'take two' on New Year's Eve. I, being an asshole, insisted it was too late. But he didn't take no for an answer.

He took me hiking to the Great Falls State Park. Per usual, hiking was our 'deep conversations time'. I communicated everything that was bothering me. It seemed like he finally understood the issue. All it took was one car ride, a bit of hiking, and we were back to being us. In love, messing with each other, and fighting every five minutes about nothing in particular. I loved fighting with Andrew about stupid things that didn't matter. I just hated those serious fights when I felt misunderstood.

After the hike we went to Wagshal's Market, my favorite place in DC. We got some bread, carrot cake, cupcakes - basically a monthly supply of carbs for an average person. We added sparkling cider to our baskets, not realizing it was non-alcoholic. We ended up mixing it with the wine we already had in the fridge. We cooked together, which was always a mess filled with more silly fighting and laughter. Finally, we sat down to eat dinner and watch a movie.

At 10 PM we celebrated the New Year… we both had to work the next day so midnight was a no-go. Believe it or not, that was the most fun first day of the year I had ever had. It was also a beautiful start to a new family tradition.

How To Get Used To Being No One?

Back in Europe, I was always proud of what I was doing. Especially in London. People asked me what my job was and I was way too excited to answer. I lived in one of the most expensive areas in the city and my dating life was thriving. I felt like I was on top of the world. London was so beautiful and completely amazing. Living there made me feel like I was the luckiest person alive - just because I was able to experience its beauty every single day.

Things changed after I came to the US. I was always a bit ashamed to admit I was an au pair. People had a set opinion about au pairs and I didn't like it. I always said I was an exchange student and hoped they wouldn't ask more questions.

It didn't get better when I became a "Pizza Girl". I know that everyone had to start somewhere and had jobs that they were kind of ashamed of. But being an immigrant was a new level of shame for me.

Don't get me wrong, I wasn't ashamed of not being American, nor being Polish. Not at all. I was very proud to talk about Polish food and how amazing Europe was. To me, it was superior to the US in so many ways. But the shame didn't come from me - it came from the outside.

It wasn't easy to live in a Trump country where every day a new law was created to prevent me from living here. Building walls, raising the green card application fee to over a thousand dollars more, and extending the wait time for specific documents and permits.

Within those few months of applying for a green card, every day I was reminded that I was no one here. I didn't have any rights, even the basic ones like having a driving license or working. I couldn't even leave this country without the risk of not being able to come back. Without the work permit, I couldn't get a new Social Security Card and I couldn't legally change my last name without it.

Getting used to this new reality wasn't easy for me. I was way too ambitious and deeply believed in myself. I couldn't just sit around and accept that I lost all of my rights just because I fell in love. I wanted to scream and shout. I cried more than ever in my life. I was angry like never before and so frustrated that I decided to write a book about it. I also kept complaining and thinking of my escape plans. At some point I stopped looking for flights to London though, so that was some progress, I guess.

I was lost. My life was a mess and I honestly didn't know what I wanted besides being over with that whole process. Every day I convinced myself that it was going to be a good day and then shit happened. I kept finding myself crying in my fiancé's arms, angry at him when I actually was angry at everything but Andrew.

I sucked at this. I sucked at being no one. I sucked at not having any rights and not having a fancy job I could brag about. I sucked at being Andrew's fiancée just because I felt ashamed of who I was in the first place. I felt ashamed every single time I had to ask Andrew for yet another document for my green card application. It made me feel dependent and I hated it.

I felt like the US government took all of my rights away and threw them away. There were so many human rights that in my opinion were being violated by immigration laws.

So how to get used to being no one? You don't. You fight. You're more than that. Even if the whole country is trying to prove you wrong.

My Big Fat American Wedding

While organizing an American wedding, I very quickly realized that the "go big or go home" approach might get some people into a lot of trouble."Some people" was me. I was the problem. Somehow we found ourselves a couple of months away from MY dream wedding and still had no idea if we could afford it.

Planning a wedding was definitely my thing. I had always loved planning, organizing, and ordering people around… and I wondered why some people couldn't stand me. I was also a bit of a perfectionist and a dreamer. Add all of that up, and we've got a Blue Ridge Mountains wedding in a beautiful cabin for over 100 people. Only three hours away from where we actually lived. No biggie, could be much worse.

After booking the venue I was very excited to organize everything, come up with new ideas, and have the most original wedding ever.

That didn't last long. First was the dress. I got an amazing princess-y ivory dress that made me feel like the prettiest girl in the world. It was expensive but I thought it was totally worth it. The corset hugged my body tightly and all the little white flowers made it look unreal - like straight out of a fairy tale.

Reality caught up with me quickly though. After buying a car and paying a $5000 deposit for it, I realized there was no way I could have both - it was either the car… or the dress.

I loved my perfect princess dress so much, but at the end of the day I knew I needed a reliable car more than an expensive piece of clothing. Even if that piece of clothing was my dream wedding dress. Fortunately, I could return it within 30 days of the purchase, so with a broken heart (and after loads of whining), I shipped it back.

Soon enough I got a new dress, much cheaper than the previous one. I got it on sale from the same brand, but from the previous season. It was still amazing and beautiful, and most importantly - it was 70% off. It wasn't the same, but it was mine. All I could do was to make the best out of the situation. We were poor but good-looking. You can't have it all, I guess.

Pretty much the same thing happened with our wedding cake. We had this awesome idea of having a travel themed cake. With the world map on one of the tiers, the sky on the other one, suitcases, little planes and things like that.

We even went to the cake tasting which was really cool. We felt so grown up. The guy drew a few cake options for us and let us choose a different flavor for every single tier. All of it was so exciting! Until they followed up with the predicted costs of our dream cake. They said that as long as we picked it up and they didn't have to drive it all the way to the mountains, it would be only $1300… For a cake. Over a thousand dollars for a cake. Which was more than the au pair's monthly salary.

We decided to go with cupcakes instead! My favorite bakery, which didn't offer any type of wedding services, sounded like a perfect alternative. Not putting "wedding" in front of the "cupcakes" meant they wouldn't charge us an extra thousand dollars for nothing.

Last but not least… flowers. That was the nail in my wedding coffin. I didn't want anything too crazy, since I was never a person who'd spend a fortune on them. Out of "flowers and chocolates", I was the chocolates type of girl. I told the florist I'd like something simple and spring-themed since it was going to be a spring wedding. He said he understood, and then sent me a bunch of questions that I answered. I was pretty sure it was clear that I was not willing to sell my soul just for a perfect bouquet. Then he got back to me with the estimate. I opened the email and tried to see the price hidden in between fancy words for fancy flowers. There it was… Apparently, my "simple" idea was worth $1702. I did my best not to reply with:

"Dude, do you know what I could do with $1702??? I could buy a few bouquets from Target, add some extra for the tables and I'd have $1500 left. Which is the perfect amount for our monthly rent!"

Instead, I just decided to ghost him as any mature 23-year-old bride would do.

Organizing a wedding wasn't as easy and magical as I expected it to be. Even if I wasn't that girl who was crazy about the flowers or what band was going to play our first song… I was still that girl who wanted a perfect wedding and a perfect dress. I was fine with the poor version of it as long as all of my friends and family came to admire me and be there for me. Just one day in a pretty dress with people saying how beautiful I looked. Oh yes, and Andrew was supposed to be there too.

Also, I was struggling with the guest list. I didn't think I'd care if my grandma or drunk uncles were going to be there but then I realized - I did care. Knowing that we'd spent all that money, had let our lives be overtaken by it, and that we'd be talking about this day for years… it was weird to think that only my parents, brother and a couple of au pair friends would be there. No high school friends, no extended family. Not even my favorite cousin. All of them had calculated that it was too expensive to be there for me.

And I got it. I couldn't expect people to spend all of their savings just to party with me for one night in some small town in the Blue Ridge Mountains in Virginia. Believe me, I could understand. But it didn't mean it hurt less.

Still, I was excited. Finally, I had a chance to see some of my friends and my family again. Lola and Susana were coming and honestly, the two of them were more important to me than my whole family altogether. I kept telling myself it was about the quality of people, not the quantity. Plus, everyone from Andrew's side was going to be there, even people I didn't know yet. Almost everyone we loved and cared about was going to be there for us. All of them in one room - simply celebrating our relationship. What more could we ever have wanted?

Who cared about all the fancy things that cost ten times more than they should just because they were meant for a wedding? I think that a lot of people forget that "wedding" is just a different word for "party".

I should've remembered that before paying for that "perfect" venue or buying that "perfect dress"... Oh, wait, screw that! We could have gotten married in an Olive Garden for all I cared, but I had already given up one wedding dress - there was no way I was giving up another one. After all, what would be the point of a wedding if I didn't look like a princess?

Isn't It Romantic?

I knew that when I married Andrew, he would become my "sponsor". I loved how the American government took any kind of romance out of our relationship. They put us in a box with all the other green card marriages since, to them, we were all the same.

The USCIS wanted us to prove that we loved each other. That we weren't getting married because I was a calculated European whore who was using Andrew to stay in the most amazing country in the world that was the United States of America.

To prove that we are madly in love, we needed: birth certificates, passports, our marriage certificate, and tax returns for the past three years. Also, they wanted other financial documents that American people had, but I had no idea what they were and Andrew didn't feel like getting them. Photos of the two of us spending time with each other, plus some with our friends and family. Receipts, bills, anything that would prove we lived together and actually hung out with each other.

I wasn't sure how the immigration office expected me to get those…

"Hey, I love your son. Can I take a photo with you to prove that to the American Government?"

"Oh babe, I love you too! Let's take a picture for my green card application to share this moment with that lovely immigration worker that we don't know!"

"Hey Drew, let's book three weeks in Hawaii to prove to the USCIS that we vacation together!"

"Andrew, will you move in with me? It would look so much better in my green card application…"

Well, it didn't exactly go like this but it was hard to be serious when someone wanted me to prove my love to my fiancé. I could show them all the documentation they wanted but after all, we were real people and we had real emotions. It was quite frustrating to prove how we felt to people who couldn't care less about our feelings.

I got why they had to do that. They wanted to make sure people weren't getting married left and right just to stay in the US. I didn't know what the right way might be but the current green card process was definitely not the one.

I was convinced that Andrew and I would get through it and still be as in love as we were the very first time we met. Probably more than that. In my head, we were Romeo and Juliet and the USCIS was playing the role of our horrible families trying to break us apart. The only difference was that I already promised Andrew to live longer than him and to die no sooner than at the age of 80. So we might get a better ending after all.

All we could do during that sick process was to take it day by day. I did believe this process was dehumanizing. I felt like a criminal who wanted to get away with my crimes. The crimes being falling in love with the "wrong" person. I hated the fact that I had to go through it, and very often I didn't deal with it very well.

But then I took a look around me and I saw all the people I would've never met if I didn't decide to stay here and fight for myself… for us. I saw all the love around me and support from everyone that we cared about. Waiting for the future to happen was frustrating as hell but at the end of the day I was safe, I was loved, and I gained a new family that I loved more than anything.

I Just Wanna Go Home

Every au pair could talk for hours about homesickness. At least I could. It's funny… because when we au pairs get homesick while we're away from our home country, we talk about it and get through it. Then we come back home and realize it's not our home anymore. It's a strange place that we left behind and somehow, we found a new home elsewhere. So we get homesick again. This time not for where we are from, but for where we belong.

I was lucky enough to have more than one home in life. In the beginning, it was Poland. Then DC, and finally England. At different points in my life, I missed different homes but when I was starting my life with Andrew, there was no other place I'd have rather been than London.

Lola was trying to apply for a job over there and I was telling her everything I knew about apartments (or flats), jobs, and the places I used to visit there almost every week. Before I knew it, I had become homesick like never before. The fact that I wasn't even close to getting my work permit and I was still a "Pizza Girl" was not helping at all. I just wanted to go back "home" to my old job and move in with Lola.

In an ideal world, Andrew would have wanted to move to

England with me. We would've found a flat where we all could live together as a happy and a very dysfunctional family. In an ideal world, it would've been possible for me to travel back and forth to spend some time with my European friends. In an ideal world, I wouldn't have felt like the USA was my prison.

I was seriously going crazy. I felt like I just wanted to run away and leave everything behind. I wanted to find myself in between those South Kensington buildings again. I was homesick for my friends and the stunning architecture. I was homesick for walking around my city just for the simple pleasure of walking. I was homesick for not needing to own a car and the endless public transportation options. I was homesick for my favorite tuna bagel from the B Bagel café on Fulham Road. I was homesick for people talking about their weekend trips to a completely different country. I missed all of it and didn't know what to do about it.

Did I see my future in the US? Definitely. But at the same time, I couldn't get over the feeling that everything here was just big and ugly. It was probably because of the area we lived in and also the whole homesickness thing. But it didn't change the fact that I didn't want to be here anymore. After all the struggles and all the shame I felt - I was defeated and I just missed my other home. London wasn't perfect but at least it meant freedom. For me, the US was like a prison for immigrants just with better food.

The walls around me were closing, and since I was claustrophobic I started suffocating pretty quickly. Then I saw the window and there was a FREEDOM sign right outside. I wanted to reach for it. Still, I was holding on to the hope that at some point I'd find my strength and punch through the walls.

Dear Mr. President

When I got an email saying that the "public charge rule" went through and would be effective on February 24, 2020, I felt like someone punched me in my gut.

What was the "public charge rule"? Well, it meant that Donald Trump still didn't like immigrants, that's for sure. Which was actually quite concerning since his own wife was an immigrant. I didn't know their story but I guessed they didn't have to deal with all that immigration crap - so they had no idea how it felt. As far as I knew, Melania Trump did some illegal things while being on her visitor's visa but that didn't really matter since she married the rich guy, right?

The "public charge rule" was supposed to prevent immigrants from getting visas or green cards if they weren't in the right financial situation or had ever received some public assistance.

To be honest it didn't affect my case that much. Andrew had a good job that paid well enough for me to be able to apply without any complications. I had decent jobs before being an au pair as well. My education sucked since I never graduated from college, but still, it could've been worse. They did add about 200 pages to my application, though. That was fun.

We couldn't afford a regular immigration lawyer. Most of the immigration lawyers charged about $3,000 per case, at least. However, I didn't want to be left out with no help either. So I chose something in between. I hired an online company that cost "only" $750 per case. They helped us a lot with all the forms and other stupid stuff that I hated dealing with. That was how I found out about the new rule. They talked about it for weeks but honestly, I was hoping it would take a bit longer to get approved and that I could finish my application beforehand. We missed the deadline by a couple of weeks…

Another law that Trump's office was trying to get through was an increase of the green card application fee by almost a thousand dollars. They wanted to go from charging $1,760 to $2,750 instead. I had no idea if I was able to apply before the increase, since the new law was slowing things down for me.

It all seemed like a great attempt to make the immigration process more difficult for people who were already struggling with it. Trump said he just wanted to prevent illegal immigrants from taking advantage of the system, but we knew it was all bullshit. He was a white privileged male who hated everyone who didn't look like him or didn't come from a similar background.

The only way for people not to have any issues with the American immigration process was to have money… loads of money. But how could we expect Trump to understand our pain if he never had to face any of those issues? He thought he had the right to make decisions based only on his wealthy background. And to be honest, he did, since America gave him that right. It was hard to believe but unfortunately, that was the American reality.

The weird thing was that usually, I would've been mad at everything and everyone for giving me another obstacle to face, but not this time. I was upset, sure… but then I realized that for better or worse, that ugly American town in Northern Virginia had become my home. Trump could've done whatever he wanted to. He could come up with new rules and new ideas on how to put down the immigrants. I wasn't leaving my home or my fiancé. Donald Trump and America were stuck with me.

Green Card Marriage

So let's talk about the whole green card marriage stereotype, shall we?

We, au pairs, have a reputation. Apparently, we come to the States to find a husband and get a green card.

Do we really though…?

I had a plan, okay? I was going to become an au pair, stay for a year or two, then go to Asia and teach English. Going to Thailand was always a dream of mine. Not just for a trip, but to actually live there for a few months, possibly years. I wanted to go to its bordering countries like Laos or Vietnam. I'd travel for a few years, volunteer, and go back to London to find a job in the tourism industry or something like that.

Yet, there I was... marrying an American guy and applying for a green card. I was so annoyed that I became the stereotype I'd always hated. A part of the statistics. Just another desperate au pair who couldn't imagine leaving the United States.

We, au pairs, have a reputation… I guess it was my fault for falling for those huge brown eyes.

Some people told me before that the US was the best country in the world. What does it even mean? The best in what? There's no such thing as "the best country in the world". Just because there's Times Square, Hollywood or insane nature everywhere in between, it doesn't mean that suddenly everyone wants to live here. I mean, sure, it can be an awesome place to live but it's also the country of obesity, incredibly expensive healthcare that no one can afford, and the Donald Trump supporters.

Of course, I can't speak for every au pair in the program. However, I can speak for all the au pairs I met within my two and a half years of being an au pair, and I know that very few of us came here just to get married.

A lot of girls stay here to study and go to college. I even knew someone who got a job at the local TV station, and they sponsored her to stay in DC for three more years and work for them. A different girl got a diplomatic visa through her host family (they were diplomats) just because they loved her so much they wanted her to stay with them for another year.

There are so many au pairs who love the USA and find legal ways to stay. There are so many girls who don't think that marrying an American person is the answer to everything. Also, plenty of them enjoy their year in America and move on with their lives in their home countries.

My friends and I used to laugh at all the girls looking for American guys who were ready to marry hot European chicks and provide them with a green card. We never thought one of us would actually do it and in the end, no one did. All of my friends went back to Europe. I am the only one who stayed, which is ironic since I was the one who was ready to leave as soon as I finished my program.

Being in this situation, though, showed me the real life of a green card applicant. And you know what? It's not as easy and fun as some people might think it is.

When people say "green card marriage" they expect a pretty girl trying to use that poor guy for his citizenship. They think that she gets this amazing opportunity of living in America and then can simply divorce him and move on with her life.

However, did you know that the first green card is valid only for two years? If anyone gets a divorce before those two years are up, they could possibly lose it. The next one is valid for five years. Only after three years of marriage can the immigrant apply for citizenship. Once a citizen, a person can stay in the USA forever without being married to anyone in particular.

Each application costs anything between $500-$1,800. And don't even get me started about all the documentation needed to make it happen. I had to get a $100 evaluation that stated my high school diploma from Poland was equivalent to a high school diploma in the US.

If you ask me, getting married in the US was not fun at all. Besides the fact that I married the love of my life, I guess.

The rest? The fees, applications, documents, certificates, evaluations, work permits, travel permits, illegal jobs, fingerprinting, medical exams, more fees… The rest is a mess.

Why Girls Can Have It All

One day after I married Andrew, I dreamt I was Supergirl again. Usually, when I dreamt about things like that, I had this terrible feeling of being powerless. I knew I had the powers, and I knew I should've been using them, but then when in danger I couldn't do anything. I was powerless.

For some reason, that night my powers were working perfectly and I could fly. I could never fly in my dreams before. I only dreamt about not being able to fly.

Sometimes throughout this whole process, I asked myself… What the heck was I doing? I clearly seemed to be unhappy in the US so why would I stay here and put myself through all of this just for a guy?

Well, first of all, it wasn't just a guy. It's Andrew freaking Dearing. The funniest, goofiest, most amazing guy I had ever met.

It's true, I had a lot of awful moments that made me feel powerless and frustrated. I hated this situation that I PUT MYSELF INTO. And, at that time, I'd rather have been in Europe now.

However, I was lucky enough to have all those little amazing moments of pure joy and love that I simply couldn't leave behind. Andrew was a piece of work and drove me crazy most of the time but also, he was the only guy in the whole world who was able to steal my heart. When I met him, I had already traveled and dated my way through the world. That's how I knew there was no other person out there for me. He was the one.

Over that one year, I realized that driving me crazy was important. I seemed to lose interest very quickly so he kept it interesting for me.

But most important of all was that overwhelming feeling of love I had when I was around him. Sometimes it was just the way he looked at me. Sometimes it was how ridiculous he got. Or sometimes it was how bad I felt because he had a tough day. Whatever it was that made me feel that unconditional, breathtaking, and eye-opening love... that was the reason I'd choose him over my life in London any day.

And yes, I did feel like in some way I was letting down the strong independent woman in me. And I knew, a part of me would always feel that way. Realizing that I loved Andrew more than myself wasn't easy. A huge part of me was screaming that I was insane.

In a black-and-white world, the verdict was simple. I sacrificed everything that I ever had just for a guy. Kind of pathetic, right?

So what choices did I have going into all of this?

Black - I could easily get married, have kids, and of course, get a green card. I could become the stereotype a lot of people already thought I was and have a peaceful black-and-white life.

Or white- I could've left Andrew and move on with my life. I could go to Thailand and volunteer there for a year and go back to London afterward. I could've focused on myself, no love necessary.

Instead, I chose GREY - I got an illegal job, I was writing a book, and I couldn't wait to legalize my company. Every week I drove for over an hour in traffic just to take the hostel tourists for a tour as a volunteer. I was organizing the wedding of the century - at least that was what I believed - and I forced everyone to come and party with me in Nashville again.

Maybe you couldn't call it a successful career at that time. Maybe it wasn't an achievement yet. But if I didn't stay with Andrew, I wouldn't have done any of those things. While an illegal job was not something to be proud of, I still appreciated the fact I was able to move on from childcare. And how many people could say they were a published author? Or that they volunteered in the capital city of the United States?

I didn't leave London for no reason. I left because I wanted to experience the world. And that was exactly what I was doing. Just a bit differently than I could ever imagine.

It's so easy to say that a girl sacrifices everything for a guy. It's so easy to judge women for falling in love. It's so easy to overlook how amazing we are outside of our relationships.

My host mom used to say to me:

"You're married. You're done."

At that time, I wasn't even engaged yet. I was just very in love and excited about the possibility of my future with Drew. I had only started thinking of staying in the US for longer than I expected, and the last thing I needed to hear was that I "was married" or "done". Yes, my time with them turned out to be a bit different than everyone expected but why did it have to be a bad thing?

She kept saying she knew I was "done with them" but at that time I wasn't - not yet...

It came to the point where my birthday wishes from her were:

"Happy engaged birthday!"

Like I didn't deserve to get regular wishes anymore. I got engaged. In her opinion, there was nothing more to me anymore.

I was proud of my relationship with Drew. I was also proud of every single idea, charity work, illegal job, or stupid Instagram post within the incredibly challenging year. Yes, I was different than when I got to the States for the first or even the second time.

Yes, sometimes it was difficult to feel like myself with all these obstacles being thrown at me. Sometimes it was easy to let the negative emotions get the best of me.

Yet here you are, reading this story. I must have done something right. While writing it, I felt stronger than ever before. I accomplished one thing I thought I never would. I became an author. In many ways, our love inspired me to be a writer.

My host mom told me I was done... but I was only getting started.

Epilogue

The wedding came faster than I could ever have imagined. We changed things around, cut down the costs, talked about it a lot and finally, we managed to decrease our budget to the point we knew we could afford it. The funny thing is, it didn't matter because somehow we had managed to plan it for the very first week of COVID.

That didn't stop our closest friends from coming to celebrate with us, though. Susana flew in from Poland, Lola from London where she lived at the time, and Aroa brought her Au Pair friend. Abby and her boyfriend, who were Andrew's friends from school, came along. I met her only a couple of months before the wedding but it didn't stop us from becoming best friends within seconds. And Steven… Well, he showed up.

We drove all the way to Nashville in the middle of the night just so we could see all the bars closing as soon as we arrived. Yes, our bachelor/bachelorette party was being shut down by the US Health Department (or whoever was shutting down the whole country that week). Of course, that didn't stop a bunch of twenty-somethings from getting drunk for multiple days in a row. As long as we had Airbnb and the grocery stores were open, we were FINE.

Okay, not entirely since I was going through a huge mental

breakdown. Some people may have thought I was having cold feet but that wasn't it. I never had any doubt I wanted to marry Andrew. I was having a complete major freak-out because my dream wedding was getting canceled - and we had kind of been lying for months… We had been married since October 26th.

We eloped… didn't tell even one person. Drove to Winchester, VA, and had a guy marry us in his beautiful backyard forest. We thought we would get away with it by just "getting married" in March, but then the world shut down. Although, we were having so much fun with our friends… I was upset, disappointed, and missed London like never before. I was tired of the whole green card process and didn't know if I had it in me to continue having no legal rights; God only knew for how much longer. This was honestly the lowest point in our relationship. I felt like we were about to break up and everyone could feel the tension.

Then we got back home. After days of drinking, everyone was feeling like shit (or we all possibly had COVID). We had to face the truth. There was no wedding and we were already married.

"We will just tell them the truth," Andrew said to me. 'Them' meaning his parents.

"We can't tell them we've been married for months! Your mother will hate me!"

We didn't want to wait to schedule a new date either. I was definitely not going to keep lying about being married for another half a year. We were screwed.

And that's how we decided it would be a great idea to elope… again. We couldn't have a wedding, we couldn't tell anyone (besides the ten of our closest friends from the bachelor road trip), so we had to fake it. That seemed like the most reasonable idea.

Andrew wouldn't let me wear my big puffy princess-y wedding dress because he wanted to wear jeans. I kept telling him we would look cute, you know, a throwback to our first date, but he decided to be an asshole about it. Years later, after reminding him about it in countless fights, he admitted that he should've let me wear my ridiculous dress. Just for the record, he also admitted he was an asshole for crushing my princess wedding dreams.

At the same time, he was completely right to wear jeans to a fake elopement on Shenandoah Skyline. I wore the dress from that Vegas night when we almost got married. Did I wear a cute white lace dress on purpose that night? A coincidence, I suppose. I brought my veil with me, but who knew that veils don't just hold onto your head with no extra help, in very windy mountains?

The wedding day was stressful just like that whole week. We were done. We wanted to get it over with. I cried from frustration because I was still being a brat about not having my dream wedding. We were fighting. Then we had Andrew's dad "marry" us and we got takeout pizza and ate it in the parking lot due to the new COVID safety rules. It sucked. Our second elopement sucked.

And I have to admit, the first one wasn't that great either because I was so incredibly sick and my host family kept texting me to ask if I could work the next day. I was sick on both of our wedding nights. We were beyond frustrated - life was getting in the way every time we were trying to get married. You'd think our marriage was doomed…

But it wasn't. I decided that if I didn't get my dream wedding, I was getting a dog. Mila Jane Dearing came to our home just a week after our fake elopement. Sorry, second wedding. We spent all spring and summer playing basketball in a small park by Abby's house with her boyfriend Max, and Steven. We had food from my "pizza girl" job way too often and watched a full season of "Love is Blind" in two days. We were broke because each of us lost our jobs at one point. The world seemed to be falling apart but somehow, we got stronger. It almost felt like we were dating again. Just two kids, with way too much time on our hands, enjoying each other's company. Before I knew it, Virginia and our little family became the home I had always been looking for.

3 Years Later…

Life didn't go as planned. We had three years of a beautiful marriage until Andrew died in a motorcycle accident a day before our third anniversary.

Looking back through this book I couldn't be more grateful. For the love we shared and for me writing it all down. My memory sucks these days. It's hard to remember everything. Sometimes I only remember the bad things. How unappreciative and selfish I was when Drew was trying his best to make me smile.

We weren't perfect. Not even close. I regret many things, but not this. Writing about our love, taking way too many pictures… that's all that I have left. I miss him every single day to the point where I start to wonder whether I just imagined him. This book, and everything else I wrote about us, is proof not only that we existed, but also that we loved each other. A lot.

I never opened MartinaTravels but I did write some travel blogs for fun. Unfortunately, the reality of it was that we needed money and had to be practical. I don't want to say it was a mistake. We did our best with the hand we were dealt. However, if I could do it all over again, I'd be far less practical and try to be more… in love, I guess.

We created a family, though. We adopted Mila and after her came

Morty, Luna, and Emmie. Two dogs and two cats. We fostered around 10 animals and found them their forever homes. After Andrew's death, I adopted Sophie, the kitten. Currently, I'm fostering two puppies which was a horrible idea because I might end up adopting one of them too. Andrew would be so mad… but he'd love all of them just like he loved the first 4. We totally overdid it but at the same time, we were surrounded by love and the sense of family I never knew I wanted in my life. This family is the best thing that has ever happened to me.

Thank you to everyone who has been a part of our story from the very beginning, or even the middle. To those people who knew Andrew and helped me keep his memory alive, I just hope you know it matters. It's everything to me. People deserve to know Andrew. And Andrew deserves to live forever… in our hearts.

"Drew, unspoken love" coming soon.

Favorite
Spot List

1. B Bagels - Fulham Road, London
2. Battersea Park - London
3. Lincoln Memorial at night - Washington, DC
4. Word War I Memorial - Washington, DC
5. Cactus Cantina - Washington, DC
6. Baked and Wired - Georgetown, Washington, DC
7. Don Taco - Alexandria, VA
8. Java Grill - Alexandria, VA
9. El Agave - Warrenton, VA
10. Millers All Day - Charleston, SC
11. The Palace of Fine Arts - San Francisco, CA
12. New York New York Hotel - Las Vegas, NV
13. Santa Monica Pier - Santa Monica, CA
14. Bru's Wiffle - Santa Monica, CA

15. Cabo Cantina - Hollywood Blvd, Los Angeles, CA
16. Front Street Pizza - Brooklyn, New York, NY
17. Ellen's Stardust Diner - Manhattan, New York, NY
18. Brooklyn Bridge - New York, NY
19. Japanese Walk - Honolulu, HI
20. Kimen Ramen - Annandale, VA
21. Chateau de Chantilly - Chantilly, VA

coming soon...

Love, Death and In Between

Drew, unspoken love

also visit...

drewsbookstore.com

Printed in the USA
CPSIA information can be obtained
at www.ICGtesting.com
CBHW030828051223
2151CB00007B/12

9 798988 989929